ESSENTIALS OF
FORENSIC SCIENCE

Blood, Bugs,
and Plants

ESSENTIALS OF
FORENSIC SCIENCE

Blood, Bugs, and Plants

R. E. Gaensslen

SET EDITOR
Suzanne Bell, Ph.D.

Facts On File
An imprint of Infobase Publishing

BLOOD, BUGS, AND PLANTS

Facts On File, Inc.
An imprint of Infobase Publishing
132 West 31st Street
New York NY 10001

Library of Congress Cataloging-in-Publication Data

Gaensslen, R. E. (Robert E.)
    Blood, bugs, and plants / R. E. Gaensslen.
        p. cm.—(Essentials of forensic science)
    Includes bibliographical references and index.
    ISBN-13: 978-0-8160-5509-8
    ISBN-10: 0-8160-5509-2
    1. Forensic biology. I. Title
    QH313.5.F67G34 2008
    363.25—dc22   2007051763

Facts On File books are available at special discounts when purchased in bulk quantities for businesses, associations, institutions, or sales promotions. Please call our Special Sales Department in New York at (212) 967-8800 or (800) 322-8755.

You can find Facts On File on the World Wide Web at http://www.factsonfile.com

Text design by Erik Lindstrom
Illustrations by Richard Garratt

Printed in the United States of America

MP FOF 10 9 8 7 6 5 4 3 2 1

This book is printed on acid-free paper.

CONTENTS

Preface   ix
Acknowledgments   xiii
Introduction   xv

1 OVERVIEW   1

Forensic Science and Criminalistics—How Blood, Bugs,
  and Botanicals Fit In   1
Hans Gross (1847–1915)   4
Applications of Forensic Biology and DNA Typing   8
Blood Patterns   9
Forensic Entomology: What Bugs Can Say in Death Cases   10
Botanicals: Forensic Botany   12
Forensic Biology, Forensic Botany, and Forensic
  Entomology Today   13
The Denise Johnson Case   14

2 HISTORY AND PIONEERS   16

The Very Old Days   16
The Old Days: Blood Types and Other Genetic Factors   21
Dr. Lattes's Forensic Blood-Typing Cases   26
ABO Blood Typing and Inclusion   28
ABO Blood Typing and Exclusion   30
The Old Days to Nowadays: Milestones in Genetics   37
Using Isoenzyme Types to Include and Exclude
  Bloodstain Sources   38
DNA Is the Genetic Material   44

T 41915

Nowadays: The DNA Era   45
The Narborough Murders   48

3 DNA AND GENETICS   51
Basic Principles of Inheritance   52
Structure and Function of DNA   55
Mitochondria and Mitochondrial DNA   61
Population Genetics   63
Methods Used to Manipulate and Analyze DNA   65
Concluding Remarks   74

4 BLOOD AND BODY FLUIDS:
   PRELIMINARY TESTING   75
Principles of Handling Evidence   75
Preliminary Examinations: Searching, Identification,
   and Species Testing   77
Sexual Assault Evidence Collection Kits   82
Blood Patterns   89

5 DNA TYPING   95
Preparing DNA for Typing from Biological Evidence   95
Three Generations of DNA Typing   100
Real-Time PCR   101
Mitotypes and Y-Chromosome Markers   111
DNA Profile Databases   115
Applications of DNA Profiling   118
DNA Case Backlogs   120
Identification of the Unknown Soldiers   130
A Peek into the Future: SNPs   131

6   **BUGS AND PLANTS**   **132**

    Forensic Entomology   132

    The Erich Seebeck Case   138

    Forensic Botany   140

    Two Elderly Women in Indiana   140

7   **THE FUTURE**   **146**

    Different DNA Typing Methods: The Implications

       of Technology Changeovers   146

    Reducing Backlogs: DNA Automation and Robotics   147

    Enlarging DNA Databases: The Trade-offs between

       Law Enforcement and Civil Liberties   148

    Field Instruments: DNA Typing at the Scene?   149

    Expanded Use of Entomology and/or Botanicals   150

Glossary   151

Further Reading   162

Index   167

PREFACE

Forensic science has become in the early 21st century what the space race was in the 1960s—an accessible and inspiring window into the world of science. The surge in popularity that began in the later part of the 20th century echoes a boom that began in the latter part of the 19th century and was labeled the "Sherlock Holmes effect." Today it is called the "C.S.I. effect," but the consequences are the same as they were a century ago. The public has developed a seemingly insatiable appetite for anything forensic, be it fiction, reality, or somewhere between.

Essentials of Forensic Science is a set that is written in response to this thirst for knowledge and information. Written by eminent forensic scientists, the books cover the critical core of forensic science from its earliest inception to the modern laboratory and courtroom.

Forensic science is broadly defined as the application of science to legal matters, be they criminal cases or civil lawsuits. The history of the law dates back to the earliest civilizations, such as the Sumerians and the Egyptians, starting around 5000 B.C.E. The roots of science are older than civilization. Early humans understood how to make tools, how to cook food, how to distinguish between edible and inedible plants, and how to make rudimentary paints. This knowledge was technical and not based on any underlying unifying principles. The core of these behaviors is the drive to learn, which as a survival strategy was invaluable. Humans learned to cope with different environments and conditions, allowing adaptation when other organisms could not. Ironically, the information encoded in human DNA gives us the ability to analyze, classify, and type it.

Science as a formalized system of thinking can be traced to the ancient Greeks, who were the first to impose systematic patterns of thought and analysis to observations. This occurred around 500 B.C.E. The Greeks organized ideas about the natural world and were able to conceive of advanced concepts. They postulated the atom (from the

Greek word *atomos*) as the fundamental unit of all matter. The Greeks were also among the first to study anatomy, medicine, and physiology in a systematic way and to leave extensive written records of their work. They also formalized the concept of the autopsy.

From ancient roots to modern practice the history of forensic science winds through the Middle Ages, alchemy, and the fear of poisoning. In 1840 pivotal scientific testimony was given by Mathieu-Joseph-Bonaventure (Mateu Josep Bonaventura) Orfila (1787–1853) in a trial in Paris related to a suspected case of arsenic poisoning. His scientific technique and testimony marks the beginning of modern forensic science. Today the field is divided into specialties such as biology (DNA analysis), chemistry, firearms and tool marks, questioned documents, toxicology, and pathology. This division is less than a half-century old. In Orfila's time the first to practice forensic science were doctors, chemists, lawyers, investigators, biologists, and microscopists with other skills and interests that happened to be of use to the legal system. Their testimony was and remains opinion testimony, something the legal system was slow to embrace. Early courts trusted swearing by oath—better still if oaths of others supported it. Eyewitnesses were also valued, even if their motives were less than honorable. Only in the last century has the scientific expert been integrated into the legal arena with a meaningful role. Essentials of Forensic Science is a distillation of the short history and current status of modern forensic science.

The set is divided into seven volumes:

- ☑ *Science versus Crime* by Max Houck, director of research—forensic science, West Virginia University; Fellow, American Academy of Forensic Sciences; formerly of the FBI (trace evidence analyst/anthropologist), working at the Pentagon and Waco. This book covers the important cases and procedures that govern scientific evidence, the roles of testimony and admissibility hearings, and how the law and scientific evidence intersect in a courtroom.

- ☑ *Blood, Bugs, and Plants* by Dr. R. E. Gaensslen, professor, forensic science; head of program and director of graduate studies, University of Illinois at Chicago; Distinguished Fellow, American Academy of Forensic Sciences; former editor of the *Journal of Forensic Sciences*. This book delves into the many facets of forensic biology. Topics include a historical review of forensic serology (ABO blood groups), DNA typing, forensic entomology, forensic ecology, and forensic botany.

☑ *Drugs, Poisons, and Chemistry* by Dr. Suzanne Bell, Bennett Department of Chemistry, West Virginia University; Fellow of the American Board of Criminalistics; and Fellow of the American Academy of Forensics. This book covers topics in forensic chemistry, including an overview of drugs and poisons, both as physical evidence and obtained as substances in the human body. Also included is a history of poisoning and toxicology.

☑ *Trace Evidence* by Max Houck. This book examines the common types of microscopic techniques used in forensic science, including scanning electron microscopy and analysis of microscopic evidence, such as dust, building materials, and other types of trace evidence.

☑ *Firearms and Fingerprints* by Edward Hueske, professor of criminalistics, University of North Texas. Distinguished Member of the Association of Firearm and Tool Mark Examiners; Fellow, American Academy of Forensic Sciences; emeritus member of American Society of Crime Laboratory Directors (ASCLD). This book focuses on forensic firearms evidence and fingerprint evidence and their use in the solution of crimes.

☑ *Crashes and Collapses* by Dr. Tom Bohan, J. D.; Diplomate, International Institute of Forensic Engineering Sciences; Founders Award recipient of the Engineering Sciences Section, American Academy of Forensic Sciences. This book covers forensic engineering and the investigation of accidents such as building and bridge collapses; accident reconstruction, and transportation disasters.

☑ *Fakes and Forgeries* by Dr. Suzanne Bell. This book provides an overview of questioned documents, identification of handwriting, counterfeiting, famous forgeries of art, and historical hoaxes.

Each volume begins with an overview of the subject, followed by a discussion of the history of the field and mention of the pioneers. Since the early forensic scientists were often active in several areas, the same names will appear in more than one volume. A section on the scientific principles and tools summarizes how forensic scientists working in that field acquire and apply their knowledge. With that foundation in place the forensic application of those principles is described to include important cases and the projected future in that area.

Finally, it is important to note that the volumes and the set as a whole are not meant to serve as a comprehensive textbook on the subject. Rather, the set is meant as a "pocket reference" best used for obtaining an overview of a particular subject while providing a list of resources for those needing or wanting more. The content is directed toward nonscientists, students, and members of the public who have been caught up in the current popularity of forensic science and want to move past fiction into forensic reality.

ACKNOWLEDGMENTS

I thank Dr. Suzanne Bell, the set editor, for providing me with the opportunity to be one of the authors in this interesting set of books on the forensic sciences. She brings a marvelous and infectious sense of enthusiasm for forensic science and encouragement to the project. I also thank Frank K. Darmstadt, executive editor, Dorothy Cummings, project editor, and the rest of the staff at Facts On File, who guided the process along.

Tiffany Vasquez, an alumna of the M.S. program at the University of Illinois, gathered up many photos and artwork. She is currently a full-time DNA analyst at the Office of the Chief Medical Examiner (OCME) in New York City. Artwork and figures are always a difficult aspect of creating any book that is designed to be a teaching aid. Another graduate of the M.S. program, Sara Melton, also contributed to collecting the photos and artwork. She is also currently employed as a DNA analyst at OCME, New York City. Their help was essential in illustrating this book.

Dr. Neal Haskell, a colleague who is a forensic entomologist in Rensselaer, Indiana, read and provided critical comments on the sections on forensic entomology.

Dr. David Stoney, a colleague who was until recently a clinical professor of forensic sciences at the University of Illinois at Chicago and director of the McCrone Research Institute in Chicago, provided a figure for the section on botanical evidence.

Some drawings were inspired by and adapted from graphics on the Access Excellence @ the National Health Museum Web site located at the following URL: http://www.accessexcellence.org/RC/VL/GG.

INTRODUCTION

Blood, Bugs, and Plants is one volume in a multivolume set, Essentials of Forensic Science, that explores several core biological areas of modern forensic science. In regard to this volume entomology ("bugs") is a specialty that uses knowledge about insect life cycles to inform death investigations. Botanicals ("plants") is a specialty that looks at plant materials as evidence in cases. The "blood" part is the largest part of the book. It covers the identification of blood and body fluids (determining their origin as human or animal), DNA typing, and also blood-spatter patterns.

The book is divided into seven chapters. Chapter 1 is an overview that briefly introduces each of the specialty areas that will be covered and also presents some basic concepts in forensic science that will help the reader understand how these biological sciences can shed light on issues in legal cases. Besides identifying and DNA typing of blood and other body fluids—the main topic of this book—another aspect of bloodstain evidence is the blood patterns at violent crime scenes, which can be helpful in reconstructing the events. All the material on blood and the material on plants are part of a large forensic science specialty called criminalistics. This specialty can be thought of as the collection of scientific activities that take place in a modern forensic science laboratory. Criminalistics and some of its principles are described in chapter 1.

Chapter 2 looks at the history of the scientific subjects that are important to blood, bugs, and plants, introducing their pioneers and the contributions they made. Some threads in the analysis of blood evidence go back centuries, to the time of Dr. M. J. B. Orfila (1787–1853). He was the first person who published papers on the forensic analysis of blood and physiological fluids. During much of the 20th century forensic scientists attempted to do genetic analysis of blood, based on blood types and special blood enzymes, in order to help decide whose blood it might be. Perhaps the major pre-DNA pioneer was the Nobel laureate Karl Landsteiner (1868–1943), who discovered blood types. To get to the stage where forensic DNA typing could be a reality required advances in both molecular biology and genetics. Milestones in both these areas are presented and discussed in chapter 2, and some of the scientists involved in major discoveries are introduced as well. Forensic DNA analysis did not come along until the 1980s. The work of Sir Alec Jeffreys in introducing forensic DNA typing to the world brings us up to the present time. The development of DNA science has gone hand in hand with the development of genetics. Chapter 2 introduces some of the early contributors to genetics—who worked with plants, fruit flies, and bread mold—and discusses their work. Many of the developments in molecular biology (also called biochemical genetics) had to do with providing a molecular explanation for what was already known about inheritance, how traits and characteristics get from parent to child. Forensic entomology and forensic botany have a less linear, organized history than forensic blood analysis, but there are historical cases and some forensic scientists who have brought these specialties along.

In chapter 3 the scientific principles underlying DNA and genetics that form the basis for forensic analysis are introduced and described. The principles of classical genetics—the basic rules of inheritance—were discovered by the early genetics pioneers and apply to all the plants and animals on Earth. The structure and function of DNA are also discussed. The DNA in the cell nucleus is responsible for transmitting most of the information from parents to offspring, but there is a small quantity of DNA in the cell's mitochondria as well. Both nuclear and mitochondrial DNA have roles in forensic DNA analysis. The chapter describes the methods that forensic scientists use to manipulate DNA.

Chapters 4, 5, and 6 examine the analysis of physical evidence in forensic cases and how it evolved from the historical developments and the work of the pioneering scientists. Chapter 4 is about the first task in the laboratory: preliminary evidence examination and identifying blood and different physiological fluids. This testing is generally done in connection with the preliminary examination and searching of evidence. Accordingly, some principles of evidence handling are described in this chapter. Determining the species of origin of blood is also part of this identification process and is discussed here. Next, blood pattern analysis is introduced and discussed. The patterns blood forms on evidence items can help forensic scientists reconstruct the events that caused those patterns.

Chapter 5 is about forensic DNA analysis. This specialty is built on a foundation of DNA analysis for other scientific purposes. Forensic DNA analysis has already been through several generations of technology; that is, several different methods have been used, and newer ones have completely replaced the older ones. The earlier generations of DNA-typing technology are introduced and briefly described before the chapter discusses the current profiling technology in some detail. Some specialized forensic DNA techniques, such as mitochondrial DNA sequencing and Y-chromosome sequence analysis, are also introduced. Interpretation of DNA profiling results is also discussed in chapter 5. The important point regarding interpretation of results is that it is not always simple and straightforward. One of the most important impacts of forensic DNA analysis has been the ability to construct databases of people's DNA profiles. Once someone's profile is in a database, one can search the database for that profile, and the person can be identified. Whose DNA profiles should be in databases is a major public policy issue currently facing people in the United States, and chapter 5 presents some of the pros and cons involved.

Chapter 6 is devoted to forensic entomology and forensic botany—the bugs and plants. Insect life cycles are predictable, so when insects colonize a dead human body, entomologists can analyze them to help estimate the time of colonization and, thus, the time of death. Plant parts can be evidence of association between persons and particular places. Plant (botanical) evidence belongs to a category that forensic scientists call "trace and transfer" evidence. This means that small quantities (traces) can often be successfully analyzed. Such evidence is valuable in cases when it is transferred between and among objects or persons. In addition, plant materials that a person ate not too long before his or her death can help pathologists know what that person's last meal was and how long before death it may have been ingested.

Chapter 7 looks into the future. Where are forensic science and forensic technologies going? Where should they be going? What are the implications of the changes that might occur?

The book has sidebars about people, forensic issues, and case illustrations. The cases are stories of things that have happened, and they were selected to make certain points about the physical evidence analysis and conclusions—to help reinforce the text. There is a glossary that defines all the technical terms, as well as a list of notes and references for further reading and exploration.

Forensic science is interesting and fulfilling work. When it is done properly, the work is also honorable. Someone's freedom can be riding on a forensic scientist's analysis and conclusions. It has to be done carefully, correctly, and without bias. If forensic scientists assist the justice system in coming to correct conclusions, they have made a positive contribution to the good of society.

1

Overview

This chapter introduces forensic science and some of its specialty areas. Criminalistics, in particular, is discussed at length because it encompasses the "forensic science" that goes on in most of the crime laboratories in the United States. Some fundamental concepts in criminalistics are described. These are applicable to the specialty areas that are the subject of this book. The way this book's specialties fit into forensic science and criminalistics is discussed. A process of comparison characterizes most forensic examinations. Most of the book is devoted to forensic biology, and the reasons for this are given in this overview. There are descriptions of the types of casework applications to which forensic biology, forensic entomology, and forensic botany are applicable.

FORENSIC SCIENCE AND CRIMINALISTICS—HOW BLOOD, BUGS, AND BOTANICALS FIT IN

Forensic science is science applied to legal matters and cases, including criminal cases. The latter is where most people hear about the topic of forensic science. All of the popular television shows on forensic science involve crime and criminal cases. Criminal cases involve the state or the U.S. government charging someone with violating its laws.

But forensic science can also be used in civil court cases. Civil cases deal with disputes between people or between people and companies or organizations. DNA tests can be used, for example, to find out if a man is the father of a child. A document expert may be asked to examine the authenticity of someone's handwritten last will and testament. Is it the real thing? Did the person really write it? A civil case could involve a product failure. A tire on a car might fail while someone is driving along, causing an accident, and the person might take action against the tire maker. That case would likely involve a forensic expert, a tire expert.

Forensic science is also used to help support the enforcement activities of regulatory agencies. The U.S. Coast Guard, for example, can seek punishment against the operators of a tanker that spills oil in a river, sound, or harbor within U.S. waters. To make such a case, though, forensic chemists have to compare the composition of the spilled oil with that in the tanker and help show that this is the ship that spilled the oil. Another example is the work done by the U.S. Fish and Wildlife Service Forensic Lab in Oregon. This laboratory conducts tests to help enforce various regulations about importing parts from endangered animals or killing protected species within the United States.

Another application of forensic science other than for criminal cases is conducted by forensic toxicology labs that test urine for drugs. Some labs are set up primarily to help enforce the drug-free workplace rules. Other labs are set up to test race horses (or dogs) to ensure that drugs have not been used to enhance their performance. So, there are many different kinds of testing that fall under the "forensic" heading. What they all have in common is that in one way or another they have something to do with law or regulation.

Blood, Bugs, and Plants is a book devoted mainly to the issue of identifying human blood and physiological fluids, and then DNA typing them to see who may have left them. These forensic activities are usually called "forensic biology." In addition, the book discusses the use of insect life cycle stages as a means to help figure out the time since death (forensic entomology) and the use of plant materials as transfer evidence (forensic botany and palynology).

Identifying blood and physiological fluids and conducting DNA typing are very common activities in the modern forensic laboratory. Many violent crimes can have evidence with blood and body fluids. As a result many cases with this type of evidence are submitted to forensic laboratories. There are many forensic scientists in the laboratories engaged in blood and body fluid analysis activities.

Plant materials are a much less common type of evidence. Only a small number of cases are submitted to the laboratory with requests to examine the botanical evidence. Not many cases have botanical evidence. Because of this there are not very many forensic scientists who know how to analyze botanical evidence. Not many forensic scientists have training or education in botany, the science of plants. As a result forensic botany is not a significant part of the activities of forensic laboratories. When a case has important botanical evidence, a forensic laboratory might look for an outside expert, such as a university professor, to help with the analysis.

The situation with forensic entomology is somewhat similar. Very few death cases have insect evidence that might help in figuring out the time since death. It is more likely that bodies will have insect evidence if they are outside at the time of death (or moved outside soon afterward), and if they are not discovered for a day or more. These circumstances are not very common and represent only a fraction of all the deaths forensic scientists investigate. As a result there are not many forensic entomology specialists. Most forensic entomologists are employed most of the time as university professors. There is not enough case work to keep a forensic entomologist busy all the time, even in a very populous city or area. They are called upon as needed, usually by coroners or medical examiners or sometimes by attorneys preparing cases. For these reasons this book focuses more on forensic biology and DNA than on forensic botany or entomology.

Forensic biology and botany are part of a forensic specialty called "criminalistics." This word came into English from German in the 19th century. Generally it means the evaluation of physical evidence for legal purposes (a lot like forensic science). The word was coined by a European magistrate, Hans Gross (see sidebar "Hans Gross").

In continental Europe the legal system is different from that of the United States and United Kingdom. In European criminal cases there is an "examining magistrate" (like Hans Gross); he or she is responsible for conducting an investigation of the case, including ordering the forensic laboratory tests. In the United States these functions are performed by police investigators and by prosecutors. Knowing what an "examining magistrate" does in the criminal justice system makes it easier to understand why such a person as Gross would start thinking like a criminalist.

Criminalistics includes the activities and specialty areas that would be found in large, full-service forensic science laboratories. These include chemistry, biology and DNA, trace and materials analysis, and pattern evidence analysis and comparison (which includes fingerprints, firearms, tool marks, and questioned documents). Experts in areas of criminalistics are often called "criminalists." The news media sometimes confuse this word with *criminologist,* but they are not the same thing. A criminologist is a social scientist who specializes in the study

Hans Gross (1847–1915)

Hans Gross was an Austrian criminal jurist who, for part of his life, was an "examining magistrate," meaning that he was responsible for carrying out investigations in criminal cases. Among other things the examining magistrate was responsible for requesting forensic testing in a case. Gross was not a scientist himself, but he requested the scientific tests conducted on evidence, and this experience taught him to think like a forensic scientist. He wrote a major book in 1893 titled the *Handbook for Examining Magistrates, as a System of Criminalistics.* It is from this book that the word *criminalistics* came. Gross recognized that a scientific and systematic approach to criminal investigation and evidence testing was vital to a good and just case outcome. Many forensic scientists attribute the birth of modern criminalistics to the book.

During his life Gross was a professor at Chernivtsi University (in Ukraine), Prague University (in the Czech Republic), and finally at the University of Graz (in Austria). He wrote books in other disciplines, such as criminal psychology, during his lifetime as well.

of crime and criminal behavior. Criminalists are always specialists in one of the criminalistics areas noted, such as trace evidence or chemistry. But, besides being specialists, criminalists are taught to think about evidence and cases in certain ways. They understand the importance of recognizing evidence. That might sound trivial and simple, but it is not. Knowing what is important and what is just background at a scene is a skill that takes considerable experience and training to acquire. Similarly, in the laboratory, evidence items must often be searched to look for hairs, fibers, biological stains, and so forth. There is an old saying, "You only see what you're looking for," which means that something important can easily be overlooked because someone is not thinking of it or trying to find it, or is so focused on something else that the person misses the obvious. One important idea in criminalistics is to look carefully at scenes and evidence and try to find everything that is or might be important.

Besides recognizing evidence, criminalists are taught to carefully document evidence. This means keeping good records and notes. Whether at scenes or in the laboratory criminalists document evidence, and they document their examinations. Documentation of crime scenes is often in the form of photos and sketches. Documentation has to be detailed enough so that someone can go back to it months, even years, later and remember what he or she observed and found, the results of testing, and so on.

Criminalistics examinations can also involve identification of evidence items or traces and individualization of those items or traces if possible. Identification ordinarily means figuring out what something is. That might be obvious and easy (for instance, with a latent fingerprint or a paint chip), or it could require testing (for instance, with a reddish stain that might or might not be blood). In criminalistics, identification is the same as classification. The individualization part of the examination is designed to show that the evidence trace or item is unique—the only one of its kind. This cannot be done with many types of evidence, but it is an important goal.

Criminalists sometimes talk about class characteristics and individual characteristics of evidence items. Class characteristics are features of all the things in a big group, like all hairs, all fibers, all blood, all paint, and so on. These are the features that place the item into the larger group as a means to identify, or classify, it. Hairs all have common features that result in their being classified into the same group. Individual characteristics, on the other hand, are those features that distinguish the particular item from other members of the bigger group. For example, a human DNA profile can be specific to one person, or a particular composition (chemical makeup) profile might be characteristic of one or a few items of some material within a larger group. Many types of evidence cannot be truly individualized. As a general rule trace materials and chemical evidence cannot be individualized. Biological evidence often can be individualized using DNA profiling. Fingerprints, bullets and cartridge cases, and handwriting can often be individualized.

Another criminalistics activity in some cases is reconstruction. In this book this aspect of evidence analysis will come up as it pertains to blood patterns. Blood pattern analysis can help reveal the events or types of forces that produced them. Sometimes reconstructions can be done in whole cases. Scene and evidence documentation and the results of laboratory analysis are used in reconstructions.

A final point about the criminalistics specialties in the forensic science laboratory is that many of the analyses are actually comparisons between a known and an unknown specimen. A hair, a fiber, a paint chip, or a blood trace is not very useful by itself, nor are many other potential types of evidence. What is needed is a known, meaning a sample that is known to be from the suspected source of the evidence, with which to compare them. Investigators are usually responsible for obtaining or arranging for the collection of the known specimens and then ensuring that they are brought to the laboratory. To obtain known specimens for comparison investigators must have an idea about where the unknown might have originated. They must obtain known hairs from people who may have contributed the hair evidence, or known fibers from clothing or carpets or other materials, or known paint from the suspected source, or known blood from persons. In a hit-and-run case, for example, there may be a paint smear or paint chip on or near a victim or associated with the scene or a victim's vehicle. Investigators must locate a suspect vehicle in order to collect known paint for comparison. Otherwise the lab can only tell a possible make and model of vehicle (from a library of paint specimens supplied by auto manufacturers). In some circumstances, with some types of evidence, the known specimen might be produced in the laboratory. For example, if a sneaker imprint is found at a scene and the investigators are able to collect the imprint pattern by tape-lifting it, they will have to locate the sneaker they think is responsible and send it to the lab. The lab will then make knowns for comparison by inking the sole of the sneaker and making known inked impressions on a clean surface. Forensic scientists sometimes call unknown, or evidentiary, items "questioned" because they do not know (at least initially) what or whose they are; similarly, knowns may be called "exemplars."

In forensic biology the knowns are obtained from people. DNA typing of evidence produces a result (an unknown) that can be compared with a similar DNA typing from a specimen from a known person. In forensic botany knowns must be collected from the scene or from the suspected place of origin. Forensic entomology is not part of criminalistics, and it does not primarily involve the comparison of knowns and unknowns.

In any comparison between questioned and known specimens, if the two do not match the questioned item is excluded from having originated from the known item or person. This conclusion is absolute and means that the evidence did not come from the known item or person. If the specimens do match the forensic scientist must next consider what conclusion the science permits with whatever type of evidence it is. Specifically, can the scientist say the questioned and known specimens had a common origin; that is, did the questioned specimen originate from the known? This question is too complicated to discuss in detail here for all the different kinds of physical evidence, but some general rules can be noted. Fingerprints and handwriting can often be attributed to a specific person, while bullets and cartridge cases can often be attributed to a specific firearm. Blood (and physiological fluids) can often be attributed to a specific person through a DNA profile. Finally, trace evidence (fibers, glass fragments, soil, paint chips, and so on) generally cannot be individualized. Note that exclusions are just as important and valuable as inclusions. The forensic scientist's job is to evaluate the physical evidence and use the results to shed light on the case.

There are now several important databases available to forensic scientists and investigators: for fingerprints, AFIS (Automated Fingerprint Identification System); for bullets and cartridge cases, NIBIN (National Integrated Ballistics Information Network); and for DNA profiles, CODIS (Combined DNA Indexing System), the database most important to this book. With any of these items of evidence a laboratory can search a database and see if the fingerprint, fired evidence, or DNA profile has been seen before. The lab can do these searches even without a known specimen, but there is no guarantee a match for the evidence item will be found in the database. In addition, each database has what is called a "forensic file," profiles or images of evidence recovered in unsolved cases. Finding a match in the forensic file means that this case is associated with the other case through the physical evidence item, but it does not solve the case or identify the person or the gun. More about DNA profile databases is presented later.

In summary, criminalistics involves the following:

1. all the steps in recognizing, documenting, and analyzing physical evidence

2. identifying and individualizing (if possible) items of physical evidence

3. using physical evidence to reconstruct events (if possible)

The individualization aspect often involves comparing unknown (scene) items with known items to see if there are matching characteristics.

APPLICATIONS OF FORENSIC BIOLOGY AND DNA TYPING

Most of this book addresses the forensic analysis of blood and other physiological fluids and their dried stains. The first part of this analysis consists of identifying dried stains and residues as blood, semen, saliva, vaginal secretions, and so on. If a stain is identified as blood it is next tested to see whether it is human or animal. This species-testing step is ordinarily not done on physiological fluids because it is generally possible to infer human origin from context. As an example of this reasoning consider saliva traces on a cigarette filter; these are certainly human. Bloodstains or traces can of course be of animal origin. Sometimes the lab must try to find out what animal was the source of the blood.

Analysis and DNA Typing of Blood and Other Physiological Fluids

Once established as human, blood and physiological fluid stains and traces are next DNA typed to find out who may have deposited them. DNA profiling means finding out the DNA types at several different genetic loci.

Genetic loci, or different locations on the DNA, are explained later in the book. The combined set of types at the different locations is the profile. It is the profile that is actually characteristic of an individual.

Parentage Testing

Not too long after the discovery of blood types, it became clear that they were inherited. The ability to test for discrete, inherited characteristics opened the way to using genetic testing as a means of trying to establish (or disprove) parentage.

A child's mother is usually known because there is some record of the child being born to her, so most disputed parentage cases involve disputed paternity. Most of these cases are brought in family courts and attempt to establish paternity in order to give the court a basis for ordering a man to pay support for his child. Today, with DNA-typing methods the chances of falsely including a true nonfather are exceedingly small; in other words, if DNA testing results provide a high probability that a particular man is a child's father, then he almost certainly is. For the family courts a DNA parentage inclusion is equivalent to proof of parentage. By the same token DNA typing will virtually always exclude a true nonfather. This topic is discussed further in chapter 5.

Identifying Human Remains

Most societies consider it important to recognize the death of an individual and to dispose of his or her remains in a particular way. Most people die under circumstances where their identity is not in question. But in cases where deaths are sudden or unexpected, occur without any medical oversight (outside a clinic or hospital), or might involve foul play, they are investigated by medical examiners or coroners. The first step is identifying the body. Identification of remains is also one of the major goals in mass disaster situations, such as airplane crashes. The U.S. Armed Forces are likewise dedicated to identifying the remains of military personnel who die in the line of duty. Using DNA analysis to help identify human remains is discussed in chapter 5.

BLOOD PATTERNS

The interpretation of blood patterns is the reconstruction aspect of forensic blood analysis. It is distinct from identification, species testing, and DNA analysis. During violent events blood can drip from a source, or it can be spattered onto floors, walls, and objects. The patterns the blood forms on the surfaces can help a forensic scientist know what type of event caused the blood to spatter in the first place, how much energy was involved, and possibly something about the direction of a moving source and the angles at which blood droplets hit the surfaces.

Blood patterns at crime scenes are important sources of information about the events that took place there. If there is a possibility that more than one person was bleeding, the laboratory analyzes specimens of the dried blood, first, to make sure it is blood; then, to make sure it is human; and finally, to analyze its DNA profile. Blood patterns will have different meanings if there is more than one blood source. As a result the identification and individualization steps in blood analysis always precede the reconstruction step.

FORENSIC ENTOMOLOGY: WHAT BUGS CAN SAY IN DEATH CASES

Entomology is the study of insects; forensic entomology is the study of insects to help resolve legal questions. One of the most important uses of forensic entomology is to help uncover information about certain human deaths.

There are more species (different kinds) of insects than any other group of plants or animals on Earth. They make up nearly 25 percent of all the known living organisms. With so many species there is great competition among insects for food resources; therefore, different groups (families) have developed distinct feeding strategies for their survival. The different groups of insects have evolved over time by selecting specific kinds of foods, which other insects may not compete for; for instance, insects known as corn pests feed only on corn plants, while the hog louse feeds only on pigs, and so on. This process of specialization has brought about the situation where some insects select as their food resource dead, decomposing vertebrate animal carrion (the decaying soft tissues on the animals). These species of insects are known as the carrion insects, and a great many are flies.

When an animal or a human being dies, these carrion insects are attracted to the body by the chemicals that are released into the air during decomposition. Very sensitive chemical sensors on the carrion species detect these chemicals. The flies go to the body in order to lay eggs, generally in moist bodily orifices, such as the nose, mouth, or eye. After a time the eggs hatch, and fly larvae (maggots) emerge and feed on the decomposing body. When they have had enough to eat, the maggots will crawl from the body to seek a place to form a puparium (cocoon), the container for the next stage of the life cycle, the pupa. Eventually the next generation of adult insects (imago) will emerge from these puparia. All insects have this type of life cycle: egg, larva, pupa, adult.

Depending on geographical location, a variety of species of insects will be attracted to and colonize (lay eggs on) human and animal remains. Entomologists know the life cycles of these insects. When the insect forms are observed on and/or recovered from bodies, forensic entomologists can use them to "back calculate" when the eggs were laid. That time is usually very close to the time of death. The elapsed time between death and the discovery of a body is the postmortem interval (PMI).

Among the variables that can affect the precision of the calculations used to determine the time of death from insect life cycles, the most important is temperature. The speed with which the insects progress through their life cycle is temperature dependent. In addition, some of the stages are inactive during darkness, so it is important to know the number of hours of daylight that the carrion insects in a dead body were exposed to. The National Weather Service has stations throughout the country that collect temperature, daylight hours, rainfall, and other such information, but the information is collected at specific time points (such as every hour), and the weather station might be some distance from the location of the body. In some cases the time of death is very important, and the forensic entomologists may the only ones with the tools to pin it down.

It is also known that if a person has ingested drugs, and the drugs are still present in their body, the maggots feeding on that body will also ingest the drugs. The maggots can then be tested by toxicologists to see what drugs were in the body on which they were feeding. This forensic specialty area has been called entomotoxicology.

Another recent development in forensic entomology is the ability to determine human DNA types from blood-feeding insects. Insect groups such as lice, bedbugs, fleas, and mosquitoes, all of which can take a human blood meal, will have in their bodies the blood of the person they have fed upon. Thus, provided that the insects are recovered, these insects may disclose the identity of the person whose blood they were feeding on. In addition, entomologists can analyze the digestive tract contents of maggots that have fed on a decomposing human for a human DNA profile and thereby aid in the identification of the dead human. If a body was left for a time at the death scene and a maggot infestation resulted, maggots left behind after the body was moved from that scene could be used to identify the victim by DNA analysis of the maggots remaining behind.

BOTANICALS: FORENSIC BOTANY

There are at least two different ways plant materials can be useful as forensic evidence. One way—perhaps the most obvious—is as "trace" materials. Trace evidence can be many things, including hairs, fibers, glass, soil, and cosmetics, as well as plant materials that might consist of leaves, stems, flowers, seed pods, tree bark, or pollen. Many plants reproduce by producing pollen or spores, which are released to and carried by the wind. Seeds may also be windborne, and the wind can carry leaves, stems, or other plant structures as well. Plant materials often occur on or fall to the ground and can easily be transferred to a person's shoes or clothing or to a vehicle.

Most plants have a defined geographical habitat, a limited range of territory in which they live. The presence of traces of a given plant on someone or something can help show that the person or object was within the plant's habitat area. This type of information could provide valuable investigative leads and circumstantial evidence: For example, a suspect in a crime might be associated with a crime scene in this way; or a suspect's vehicle could be associated with a crime scene; or a suspect could be associated with a crime victim by finding similar plant materials on both their clothing.

With DNA technology there may also be ways to take the presence of plant materials on a person or vehicle a step further in placing the person or vehicle at a location than is possible just using visual botanical comparisons. For instance, in a real-life case the presence of pods from a paloverde tree in the bed of a pickup circumstantially placed the vehicle at the scene of a homicide in Arizona in 1992 (see sidebar "The Denise Johnson Case").

A second way plant materials can become forensic evidence is when they are ingested by people as food. Medical examiners can sometimes judge how long someone has been dead by the extent of food digestion in the stomach. Food digests in the stomach at a known rate, and forensic doctors know about this. Sometimes the food is recognizable and can be correlated with a witness statement about the decedent's (the dead person's) last meal, helping establish time of death. Medical examiners might be able to recognize various plant materials in stomach contents, like seeds, leafy structures, or the skin from a fruit. If someone was with a decedent a short time before death, and especially if they were eating together, the witness can help the medical examiner confirm the contents of a last meal. This information can help a medical examiner determine when the person died. Plant materials that pass through the digestive system but are not well digested, and thus not very much changed, can be recognized and identified in fecal material by forensic plant experts. Forensic botany experts can recognize a plant from the structures they can see when looking at it through a microscope. Although one does not hear about this very often, fecal matter can be evidence at scenes and on clothing, and once in a while a forensic botanical examination can become important in one of these cases.

FORENSIC BIOLOGY, FORENSIC BOTANY, AND FORENSIC ENTOMOLOGY TODAY

Forensic biology specialists are criminalists. In the United States there are probably about 2,000 forensic biologists working primarily in municipal, county, state, or federal forensic science laboratories. In 2002, the latest year for which reliable survey data are available, the nation's 50 largest forensic laboratories reported having about 430 forensic biologists and DNA analysts, and there were around 400 forensic laboratories in the United States. Not all of these laboratories have forensic biology or DNA services. Forensic biologists and DNA analysts receive evidence submitted by police investigators. The evidence arrives at a laboratory along with a brief description of the circumstances of the crime it is part of and a request for certain kinds of forensic biological analysis. (All of these analyses will be discussed in detail later, in chapter 4.) There are not enough forensic biologists and DNA analysts to handle all the cases, so most larger laboratories have case backlogs.

As noted above there are very few forensic botany cases, and as a result, there are very few people who are forensic botany specialists. Forensic botanical evidence may be considered "trace" evidence. Most forensic

The Denise Johnson Case

In May 1992 the body of a woman later identified as Denise Johnson was found outdoors in the brush near some paloverde trees in Maricopa County, Arizona. Her clothing was scattered about the area, and she had been bound with cloth and braided wire. She was from nearby Phoenix and appeared to have been murdered and left at the location recently. A pager recovered at the scene led the police to a suspect, a man named Mark Bogan. The investigation developed circumstantial, but not definitive, evidence against him. One of the paloverde trees at the scene appeared to have been damaged, possibly by a vehicle. A search of the suspect's pickup, pursuant to a warrant, revealed seed pods from a paloverde tree in the truck bed.

The suspect admitted that he had picked up Johnson, who had been hitchhiking, and had sexual relations with her in the pickup. But he said he had made her get out of the truck after they had argued. He denied being at the crime scene, and he denied killing her.

Police obtained the assistance of a plant molecular genetics specialist, Dr. Timothy Helentjaris of the University of Arizona, who could compare the DNA profile of the seed pods recovered from the suspect's pickup with those of the trees in the vicinity of the crime scene. The geneticist conducted blind tests on a number of paloverde trees, and the tests showed that each exhibited a different profile. The seed pods from the pickup truck showed identical profiles (indicating that they fell from the same tree), and their profile matched that of one particular tree at the scene. This evidence went a long way toward convincing the trial jury that the suspect's pickup was indeed at the crime scene, a fact that he had denied.

The plant genetics expert in this case was a university professor. He used a DNA profiling technique called RAPD (randomly amplified polymorphic DNA) that is not regularly used in forensic labs but is common in research. It is a good technique for looking at genetic variation in organisms whose total genetic makeup, or genomes, have not been mapped or sequenced very thoroughly (as was the case with the paloverde trees). The court allowed the evidence because the expert did a good job of running his tests blind and of establishing that there was much detectable variation in the trees.

laboratories have a trace evidence section. In that section items such as hairs, fibers, soils, minerals, cosmetics traces, and so forth are examined and compared. Plant materials are examined in the trace section. There are fewer trace analysts in the forensic laboratories than there are forensic biologists and DNA analysts. Less trace evidence comes into the laboratory, so the demand for analysts is smaller. In addition, trace evidence can associate things and people, but it cannot prove the association, so police and prosecutors do not think of trace evidence as definitive like biological evidence. Some of the trace evidence analysts in forensic laboratories have some knowledge of forensic botanical evidence, but they are usually not forensic botany specialists. If a forensic botany specialist is needed, that person is usually found in a university, and his or her primary job is not forensic botany. He or she is probably a biology professor who specializes in botany and is able to do occasional forensic cases as a side interest.

Forensic entomologists are also a small group. Perhaps a dozen people in the United States can say that they are forensic entomologists. Why so few? There are not too many cases where insect evidence is available, is recognized and collected, and can help establish the time of death or possibly something about the cause or circumstances of the death. As a result there is not a big need for forensic entomologists. Most forensic entomology specialists, like forensic botanists, are university professors. They are usually doctorally qualified entomologists who do occasional forensic cases as needed. Often forensic entomologists are consulted by coroners or medical examiners in death cases. They may also be consulted by police involved in an investigation that has insect evidence, or they may be consulted by attorneys preparing cases where insect evidence has played some role.

2

History and Pioneers

Before 1800 very little of the knowledge that exists today in the fields of chemistry and biology had been assembled. Medical science was in an early stage of its development, too, in part because so little basic knowledge about biology and chemistry was then available. Even in the very old days, however, people thought about how to use knowledge of medicine and science to help figure out legal cases.

THE VERY OLD DAYS

The use of science in criminal investigations was not widely practiced until the 20th century, but there are some important early examples of the application of science to investigate crimes. Insect evidence in death investigations dates back a long time. In 13th-century China an author named Sung Tz'u wrote one of the oldest known forensic medicine books, *The Washing Away of Wrongs*. He told of a case in which a man was seriously wounded in an assault, and his slashing wounds could have been made by a sickle. In this rural area many people worked in the fields and had sickles. A magistrate ordered all the men in the village to assemble, each with his own sickle. In the warm sun flies were attracted to one particular sickle—presumably because of the blood traces still on its surface. The man who owned this sickle then confessed to the assault.

More recently, in 1855 the body of a child was discovered hidden behind a wall in a house near Paris that was undergoing renovation. At autopsy Dr. Bergeret d'Arbois noted evidence that flesh flies had exploited the body initially and that certain mites had invaded it later. He placed the time of the death in 1848, years earlier than when the body was discovered. Suspicion had initially centered on the current occupants of the house, but the insect findings pointed the investigation toward the prior occupants, who were ultimately convicted of murder. D'Arbois's reasoning, that the predictable insect life cycles could be used to estimate time of death, was absolutely correct, although he may not have gotten all the details right.

Other entomologists in Europe contributed research and cases to the growing body of knowledge in the 19th and 20th centuries. Development of the use of forensic entomology in the United States has been attributed to Bernard Greenberg, a professor of biological sciences at the University of Illinois at Chicago, in the 1970s and 1980s. Recognition and use of forensic entomology, however, may have originated decades earlier, in the 1930s. At that time Director J. Edgar Hoover of the Federal Bureau of Investigation (FBI) requested biological information on blowflies from D. G. Hall, an entomologist at the U.S. National Museum, to help determine time of death of victims of the major wave of organized crime then ravaging the United States.

Judging from the body of scientific publications, the forensic use of botanical materials in human feces appears to predate their use as transfer evidence. Accounts dating back to the 19th century document the use of microscopy to discern the plant components in human fecal material. Many of these accounts were prompted because forensic scientists were looking for ways to identify traces of fecal material. Occasionally they carried analysis a step further. The analyst compared constituents of one fecal specimen with the constituents of another and used the similarity to associate an individual with a location. The use of plant parts and pollens as transfer evidence appears to be more recent. Because this kind of evidence is encountered in casework only rarely, however, few forensic scientists have shown an interest in botanical examinations.

Some noteworthy figures populate the early history of forensic biology because of their efforts to identify blood and physiological fluids and to figure out if they were human or animal. Forensic biology came to exist because investigators and courts wanted to use scientific tests and methods to gain objective information about evidence in cases. The earliest tests to identify blood were devised by a forensic doctor, Mathieu-Joseph-Bonaventure (Mateu Josep Bonaventura) Orfila.

Orfila was born on the island of Majorca (Spain) on April 24, 1787. As a young man he immigrated to Paris, France, where he studied chemistry, went to medical school, became a forensic pathologist, and eventually dominated the legal medical scene in Paris for many years. Orfila is regarded as the father of forensic toxicology. Poisoning, especially with heavy metals such as arsenic, was fairly common in his time, and he devoted much attention to the detection of poisons in body fluids. One could equally well consider him the father of forensic biology, however. In those early days there were not so many medical subdivisions and specialties as there are today because there was not very much knowledge. The experts tended to do everything.

Orfila is recorded as the first forensic expert to think about how one might identify blood in a bloodstain. At that time experts debated over how to tell whether a bloodstain was human or animal. Despite their efforts Orfila and his colleagues would not be the ones who solved these problems. The science was just not far enough advanced in his time. To their credit, though, they realized that these were important forensic questions to ask in legal cases, and that scientific methods should be found to answer them.

Two types of tests to signal the presence of blood—preliminary color tests and crystal tests—were discovered in the late 18th and early 19th centuries. The Dutch scientist J. Izaak van Deen (1804–69) was the first to describe a color test to identify blood. In a color test chemical reagents are added to a sample from a suspected bloodstain. If this sample contains blood the chemicals react because of a component in the blood, hemoglobin, producing a characteristic color. In a crystal test a chemical is added that produces, in the presence of blood components, distinctive crystals that can be identified under a microscope. Ludwig Teichmann (1823–95) and Masao Takayama (1872–1943) developed important crystal tests. Among other names that will forever be associated with blood identification tests are Oskar and Rudolf Adler and Paul J. Utz. Some of the tests are still in use

M. J. B. Orfila is widely regarded as the father of forensic toxicology. He made many contributions to the field and also published the oldest known scientific papers on identifying blood and determining species of origin. *(National Library of Medicine)*

today, for example, the Kastle-Meyer. (These tests and how they work are described in more detail in chapter 4.)

Advances in the sciences of chemistry, biochemistry, and immunology helped other 19th- and early 20th-century forensic scientists devise methods for identifying human body fluids besides blood that are commonly

The first page from two of Orfila's publications on blood identification. These articles, from the August and September 1827 issues of the *Journal de Chimie Médicale, de Pharmacie et de Toxicologie,* are among the first ever published on the subject. *(Courtesy of the author)*

seen in casework: semen, vaginal secretions, saliva, and urine. In some forensic science laboratories cases that involve rape or sexual assault are as common as or even more common than cases involving blood. The bodily fluid that these cases most often concern is semen.

Semen consists of sperm cells (spermatozoa) and a viscous liquid in which they float (seminal fluid). Sperm cells are so small that they are only visible under a microscope. There are also chemical and immunological tests for the seminal fluid itself, apart from the sperm cells. These tests are important because some men have no sperm cells in their semen, either for various medical reasons or because they have undergone a medical procedure called a vasectomy. The forensic tests for seminal fluid can be used to identify semen even when there are no sperm cells to be found.

Vaginal secretions are usually not "identified," but they are present in vaginal swabs taken as evidence from sexual assault complainants and in drainage stains on underwear. Under the microscope these stains show large numbers of nucleated epithelial cells.

Saliva usually contains a large quantity of an enzyme called amylase. Enzymes are protein molecules in cells that speed up chemical reactions. Amylase is an enzyme that helps in the digestion of starch from food. Detecting amylase is a common way of identifying saliva in forensic laboratories. (This test is discussed in more detail in chapter 4.)

Finally, urine is usually identified (when necessary) by detecting one or more of its major component chemicals, such as creatinine or urea. Once in a while it is necessary to try to identify an unusual specimen in a forensic case, such as gastric juice (if someone threw up or got shot through the stomach) or menstrual blood. There are methods that can be used for these identifications, but they do not come up very often in routine casework.

Advances in the science of immunology laid the groundwork for forensic species tests and also for the discovery and use of human blood types. The early immunologists were interested in treating and preventing infectious disease. Once scientists and doctors understood that people make antibodies against disease agents, vaccination became possible. (Antibodies are molecules that bind specifically to another substance, called an antigen, that the immune system recognizes as a threat to the body.) Scientists also figured out how to make antibodies in animals for research and testing purposes. Paul Uhlenhuth (and, independently, August von Wassermann and Nadine Schütze) made antibodies in animals that could be used to test bloodstains to see whether they were human or animal—and, if animal, which one. Forensic scientists continued to use these immunological methods for more than 100 years, and they are still used in some labs.

THE OLD DAYS: BLOOD TYPES AND OTHER GENETIC FACTORS

Almost everyone has heard of these blood types: A, B, AB, and O. They were discovered in the first years of the 20th century by Dr. Karl Landsteiner (1868–1943) in Vienna. The blood types were the first permanent, inherited difference observed among human beings. Geneticists refer to this kind of difference as polymorphism, and the occurrence of these heritable, detectable variations in the same species (the human population in this case) is the basis for all forensic genetic testing.

Karl Landsteiner was a prolific and successful scientist who made many contributions to immunology and serology. His chance discovery of the ABO blood groups in 1900 led to his receiving the Nobel Prize in physiology or medicine in 1930. Landsteiner was awarded the Nobel Prize because of the importance of ABO blood groups in correctly matching donors and recipients for blood transfusions. *(National Library of Medicine)*

Landsteiner's ABO blood group system is very important in ensuring that people who need blood transfusions get compatible blood. It is also important in helping ensure that transplanted organs and tissues will be compatible with their intended recipients. "Compatible" means that transfused blood or a transplanted organ should not contain antibodies against the recipient's red cells or tissues. ABO blood types were discovered in the Landsteiner laboratory when it was noticed that the plasma component of one person's blood could sometimes clump, or agglutinate, the red blood cells of a second person's blood. There was a distinctive pattern to these observations among the people in the laboratory, and Landsteiner correctly reasoned that this blood cell clumping had something to do with antibodies in the plasma and corresponding antigens in the red cells. (The antigens and antibodies characteristic of the main blood types are explained later in this section.)

Landsteiner's findings are important for three major reasons. First, they explained why the blood types had to be correctly matched in order to successfully transfuse blood from one person to another. Second, Landsteiner's discoveries represent the first documented example of widespread genetic variation in the human population. Finally, they identified part of the basis for tissue transplant compatibility. In 1930 Landsteiner was awarded the Nobel Prize in physiology or medicine for his discovery. The following table summarizes the characteristics of the ABO blood group system.

Blood Type	Antigens on the Red Cells	Antibodies in in the Plasma
A	A	Anti-B
B	B	Anti-A
AB	A and B	Neither anti-A nor anti-B
O	Neither A nor B	Both anti-A and anti-B

It is now apparent that the antigens A and B, which define a person's blood type, are on the surface of a person's red blood cells. Any person can have either A or B, both, or neither antigen. The peculiar thing about the ABO blood type system is that people have antibodies in their blood plasma against the antigen they lack. Thus, people with type A blood have anti-B, type B people have anti-A, etc. These antibodies can specifically agglutinate the corresponding cells. Anti-A will clump type A red cells, anti-B clumps type B red cells, and so forth. If this agglutination (clumping) were to happen in the body, it could cause death. Within the body the antibodies can also cause the corresponding red cells to break, releasing hemoglobin and other substances into the circulation. As the liver tries to metabolize the hemoglobin, it can get overwhelmed because there is too much of it. This condition is called hemolytic anemia. It can cause jaundice (a yellowing of the skin), which can be very dangerous, even fatal. It is because a person's blood has both an antigen and the opposite antibody that ABO typing is so important in transfusions.

Not long after Landsteiner's discovery forensic scientists began to think about blood types as a way of partly individualizing bloodstains in cases. The undisputed pioneer in this work was Leone Lattes (1887–1954), a forensic doctor and blood expert in Turin, Italy. He was a professor at the Institute of Forensic Medicine there. Lattes developed a method for detecting the ABO antibodies in blood (see sidebar "Dr. Lattes's Forensic Blood-Typing Cases"), but scientists later realized that the antigens were actually more stable in dried bloodstains.

Vittorio Siracusa, another forensic doctor in Italy, described a technique for typing the ABO antigens in dried blood; the paper describing this work was published in Italian in 1923. Siracusa's technique became more widespread after it was published in English much later, in 1960, by Stuart Kind in England. This procedure is called absorption-elution. It was used for decades in forensic science laboratories throughout the world. The bloodstains were often on cloth, or they could be transferred to cloth.

When blood dries on cloth, the red cells all break, but the antigens, which are attached to the cell membrane, are still there. To find out which antigens are present through the absorption-elution technique, the analyst adds specific antibodies to the bloodstained thread. If the antigen against which these antibodies are directed is present in the

Leone Lattes was the first forensic scientist to perform ABO typing on dried bloodstains for use in legal cases. He published descriptions of his work on some of these cases and wrote a book on forensic blood typing. (*Prof. Dr. A. Fornari and National Library of Medicine*)

bloodstain, the antibodies will bind to their antigen. Excess antibodies can be washed away. Then, the specifically bound antibodies can be eluted (separated using heat) from the thread. Next, any antibodies that were eluted from the thread are added to test cells, and if any antibodies are present they will agglutinate test cells that have been added.

Other blood group systems besides ABO were discovered in the 20th century, mainly from the late 1920s through the early 1950s. Some of these are the Rh (Rhesus), MNS, Kell, Duffy, and Kidd blood group systems. A few forensic laboratories, primarily in the United Kingdom,

Dr. Lattes's Forensic Blood-Typing Cases

In 1916 Dr. Leone Lattes published two cases that illustrated the forensic value of the then new technique for ABO typing bloodstains. Lattes used a method for determining the ABO type of bloodstains that relied on detection of the specific antibodies. Although published 15 years after Landsteiner first described the ABO blood group system in human beings, this work is the first report of ABO typing of dried blood for forensic purposes.

In the first case a man returned home from a trip to another town with what appeared to be bloodstains on his shirt. His wife saw the stains and accused him of adultery during his trip. Though he vehemently denied these accusations, his wife refused to believe him. The man consulted the legal medical institute for help, and Lattes agreed to test the stains to find out whom they might match. The man thought the stains might very well be his own blood, but they could also have been his wife's or possibly beef blood from the butcher shop. Lattes determined that the stains were human, eliminating the butcher shop possibility, and that they had the same ABO group as the man (type O) but were different from that of his wife (type A). According to Lattes's account, the findings helped restore peace to this family.

In the second case a man was a suspect in a homicide. He had bloodstains on his coat, but he claimed they were the result of a nosebleed. The suspect was type O, and the victim was type A (determined at the autopsy). The stains were type O, eliminating the victim as a source, and thus exonerating this particular suspect.

Note that because the results of the stains showed a blood type different from that of the victim, the victim could be absolutely eliminated as a possible source. The fact that they had the same blood type as the suspect does not show that they came from the suspect, however, only that they came from someone with blood type O. The results are consistent with the stains having come from the suspect, but they do not prove it by a long stretch. A little less than half the population is type O.

Tests for the ABO antibodies in bloodstains are called Lattes tests. Later, methods were developed to test for the antigens, and Lattes tests became a backup or confirmatory method to determine the blood type in dried bloodstains.

typed these blood group antigens in dried bloodstains in addition to the antigens they typed in the ABO system. The technique was basically the same as that used for ABO.

A curious fact about the ABO blood types is that the antigens that distinguish these blood types can also be found in the other body fluids of about three-quarters of people. In the 1930s scientists discovered that semen, vaginal secretions, saliva, and some other body fluids can have ABO blood group substances in them; the one that a person has corresponds to his or her blood type. People who have this genetically controlled characteristic are called "secretors." (It was later discovered that a simple gene pair at a single locus controls the secretor characteristic.) About three-fourths of the population have the secretor gene and therefore have the ABO blood group substances in their body fluids. People who do not have the gene, and thus do not have the blood group substances in their fluids, are called "nonsecretors." The terms are a little misleading because the blood group substances are not really "secreted" from anywhere.

Forensic scientists were interested in ABO typing of body fluids for the same reason they were interested in it for dried blood. When there is body fluid evidence—like semen in a rape case or saliva on the filter of a cigarette or the licked flap of an envelope—the blood group of the donor can be determined if he or she is a secretor. The technique used for typing ABO in body fluids was different from the one for blood; it was called adsorption-inhibition.

The specimen is added first in adsorption-inhibition. In the "test" this would be an extract from a dried body fluid stain, the "unknown." In the "control" the specimen would be a buffer solution that is known not to contain antigen. Antiserum (antibody) is added and mixed with the specimen. If the blood group antigen corresponding to the antibody is present, the two will bind. In the next step, when test cells are added, no antibody will then remain to agglutinate the cells. Agglutination of the cells by antibody has been "inhibited" by the binding of the antibody to the antigen in the test solution. In the control the test cells are agglutinated because there was no blood group antigen present, and the antibodies are available.

Historically, an important forensic application of ABO blood typing was in sexual assault cases. Before DNA analysis was available, forensic biologists used ABO typing in semen, saliva, and other body fluids to try to include or exclude suspects in these cases. The specimens for these

ABO Blood Typing and Inclusion

In the late 1970s a woman named Cathleen Crowell-Webb reported a sexual assault in a suburb of Chicago. At the time the case was "routine"; that is, it did not differ from any of the hundreds of such cases that come into forensic laboratories every year. Crowell was found to be a type B secretor, and the suspect in the assault, Gary Dotson, was also a type B secretor.

The physical evidence in the case consisted of a visible drainage stain on the complainant's underwear. This stain was tested and shown to contain semen, and ABO typing showed that it had B and H group substances. The suspect was thus included as a possible source of the semen. After a trial at which Crowell-Webb testified that he was her attacker, Dotson was convicted of sexual assault and sent to prison. The conviction was based on Crowell's testimony, but also on the testimony of a forensic scientist about the physical evidence just described.

Six years later Crowell, by then married and called Crowell-Webb, announced at a press conference that she had lied about Dotson's involvement: She had not been sexually assaulted at all, and the semen in evidence belonged to a consensual partner. This action caused a major furor in the press and in the courts. Eventually DNA typing proved that the semen in evidence was in fact not from Dotson but from another man who was Crowell-Webb's boyfriend at the time of the alleged assault. Dotson was released from prison. Cathleen Crowell-Webb died in May 2008 at the age of 46.

In the scrutiny the case received after Crowell-Webb recanted her trial testimony, it came out that the forensic biologist who had done the original analysis had misinterpreted his findings. He had said that only a B secretor male could be the source of the semen. That is not true, as the following table shows.

If the male is	He makes	And the female is B secretor, who makes	Then the resulting mixed stain would contain
B secretor	B + H	B + H	B + H
O secretor	H	B + H	B + H
Nonsecretor	Nothing	B + H	B + H

The table shows that a male who is a B secretor could be the source of the semen found in the underwear, as the analyst said. But the source could also be a type O secretor or a nonsecretor of any ABO type. Semen from males of any of the three combinations mixed with the secretions of a B secretor female would yield the same results upon typing the mixture.

The reason this point matters is because the expert usually gives the court a percentage of the population who could be sources. Type B secretors are about 7 percent of the Caucasian population and 15 percent of the African-American population. (It is general practice to state the population percentages for different racial groups, because the blood type frequencies are different among the groups.)

But given that the source could also have been an O secretor or a nonsecretor, the sum of those three groups represents about 66 percent of the Caucasian and 85 percent of the African-American populations. Even understanding that 7 percent or 15 percent of the population is a lot of people, there is quite a difference between telling the jury that the defendant is in a population group of potential semen sources that is 7 or 15 percent versus one that is 66 or 85 percent.

This is an example of an inclusion case, the defendant was included as a potential source of the semen found in the evidence. It demonstrates two things: First, including the person as a possible source of the semen stain does not mean he is the source and, second, accurately presenting the findings to the court is important. Telling the court that only 7 percent of Caucasian or 15 percent of African-American males could have been sources was simply wrong and could well have misled the jury.

tests are collected at the time the victim registers a sexual assault complaint. A woman who complains of sexual assault is usually taken to a clinic for examination, and the examination includes collecting vaginal specimens. If tests identify semen in these specimens, they can be compared for ABO type with a suspect.

ABO analysis and comparison of specimens in sexual assault cases is complicated by two factors. One is that when the vaginal specimens are collected, they represent a mixture of the body fluids of the male and the female (assuming semen is present). Accordingly, the ABO blood group substances of both people are mixed together. The analyst has to determine the ABO type and secretor status of both people separately and then try to interpret the findings.

ABO Blood Typing and Exclusion

Let us call the people involved in this case Jane Doe and John Smith. Who they are is not important to understanding the scientific issues. In the 1980s Jane Doe reported a sexual assault in a suburban town adjacent to New York City. The clinical examination she underwent at the time included taking a vaginal swab, among other items, into evidence. Doe was a type B secretor, so she would produce blood group substances B and H. When the swab was analyzed, it showed the presence of blood group substances B and H, as well as semen.

The suspect, Smith, was later apprehended as a result of the police investigation, and Doe identified him as the man who assaulted her. Smith was tested and found to be a type A secretor, so his ABO blood typing was expected to produce blood group substances A and H. No blood group substance A was found in the evidence, however.

What did this finding mean? Did it mean that Smith had to be excluded as a source of the semen? That is almost right. Smith was excluded on the face of things, but there were still a few matters the analyst had to consider.

One such matter is variation in the ratios of blood group substances. People can produce different quantities of these blood group substances in their body fluids. For instance, the relative proportions of blood group components may be different in the same person's blood and saliva. When a person is tested to find out his or her secretor status, saliva is used. In this case the analyst had to consider the possibility that the A and H quantities could be present in different ratios in the saliva and the semen of the same type A secretor man. It was possible that an A secretor

The second potential complicating factor is that all secretors make a blood group substance called H in their body fluids. Biochemically, in the body this H blood group substance is the precursor of the A and B blood group substances. People who are type O secretors make only H. But A people make A and H (because they convert some H to A); B people make B and H (they convert some H to B); and AB people make A, B, and H (they convert H to both A and B). In addition, people who

man could have more A in saliva (enough that the lab detected it when the saliva was tested) and less in semen (so that it was not detected in the semen found in the evidence specimen). Under those circumstances the man would still be included as a possible source.

But there is no way of knowing about the A and H levels in saliva versus in semen in any given case. When a person is tested for secretor status, what the lab tests is saliva because this fluid is relatively easy to obtain and getting a saliva specimen from a person is relatively nonintrusive. Forensic scientists are almost never able to test someone's actual semen, because it is too intrusive for any court to order someone to produce such a specimen. As a result it was generally not possible to sort out these possibilities through ABO blood type testing.

A second matter affecting interpretation of lab results is what the analyst does not know. For instance, if the complainant had another sexual partner besides the person who assaulted her, the analyst would not know this unless she told the police investigators about it. Even then, the analyst would have no way of knowing whether the information was correct and true.

As a result of these uncertainties it was common, when ABO blood-typing results represented the best evidence available, for forensic biologists to state conclusions about ABO blood type results conditionally. In this case the scientist might say that the man is excluded prima facie (on the face of it) by the blood group results, but that some conditions would have to be met before the exclusion could be considered absolute.

have more than one group substance in their body fluids may not have equal amounts; that is, someone who is a type A secretor could have 1,000 times more H than A.

ABO blood typing as a forensic tool is useful to a point, but it has significant limits. For instance, "including" someone as a source of a stain in evidence based on blood-typing results does not show that this person was the true source of the stain (see sidebar "ABO Blood Typing and Inclusion).

Yet, although ABO blood-typing results do not prove that someone was the true source of a stain taken into evidence in a sexual assault, under certain conditions they might exclude a suspect or defendant as the source. Exclusion should be absolute; that is, it should mean that without question the man cannot be the source. But, exclusionary interpretations are not always so clear cut (see sidebar "ABO Blood Typing and Exclusion").

The Extent of Human Genetic Variation: Isoenzymes, Serum Protein Polymorphisms, and HLA

By the 1940s methods had been developed to separate out compounds and substances from complex mixtures. Most of these techniques fall under the general heading of chromatography. Chromatography literally means "writing with color." The earliest uses of it involved separating dyes and pigments out of mixtures. Chromatographic methods, such as paper, thin-layer, gas-liquid, and high-performance liquid chromatography, are superb and now routine methods for separating (and sometimes thus identifying or characterizing) chemicals that are not too big. Chromatographic methods generally do not work very well, however, in separating the large molecules that are so important in biology: proteins and nucleic acids.

Both proteins and nucleic acids are polymers. Briefly, polymers are big molecules made up of long chains of smaller molecules bonded together. The most important molecules in biology are polymers, sometimes called biopolymers: carbohydrates, proteins, and nucleic acids. To separate these very large molecules, another technique besides chromatography was needed. Accordingly, scientists developed a new separation technique, called electrophoresis, first to study proteins and, later, to study nucleic acids.

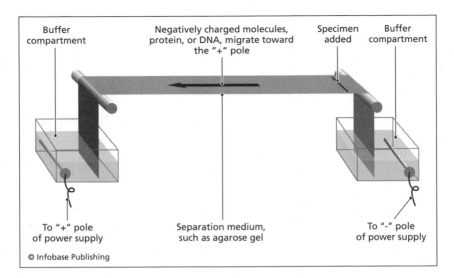

Buffer compartment   Negatively charged molecules, protein, or DNA, migrate toward the "+" pole   Specimen added   Buffer compartment

To "+" pole of power supply   Separation medium, such as agarose gel   To "-" pole of power supply

© Infobase Publishing

Electrophoresis. Proteins and DNA can be separated according to their net electrical charge and their size by this technique. The inert medium, on which separation takes place, can be paper, cellulose acetate, or a gel such as agarose.

Electrophoresis can separate large molecules that have an electric charge, and both proteins and nucleic acids have a charge. The electrophoresis process uses two buffer compartments that are separated by the buffered separation medium, as illustrated in the figure. (A buffer is a solution that resists change in pH.) Each compartment is connected to opposite poles of a power supply, and a current is set up in the medium. Negatively charged molecules move through the medium toward the positive pole, while positively charged molecules move toward the negative pole.

In forensic work electrophoresis separation media include hydrolyzed starch, agarose, and polyacrylamide. These materials can form gels (the consistency of Jell-O) that can then be used for protein and nucleic acid separation. The cells and tissues scientists want to study contain many different proteins. To study any specific one it has to be possible to separate it from all the others. The figure shows an agarose gel immersed in the buffer solution. This procedure, called submarine electrophoresis, is commonly used to separate DNA fragments. The agarose or other medium does not have to be immersed. The medium only has to be connected to the two buffer compartments so that electric current can flow from one side to the other.

Proteins are important in living systems because many of them are enzymes, the body's catalysts. Catalysts speed up chemical reactions. Without the enzyme catalysts to keep the body's vital reactions going at a high enough rate, life would be impossible. Proteins are polymers composed of building blocks called amino acids. About 20 different amino acids are the building blocks of human proteins. Since they can be linked together in almost any order, and since the proteins can be of various sizes, there is a huge number of possible different proteins. As discussed below in more detail, the sequence of amino acids in proteins, and thus protein structure, is under the control of DNA. Although the proteins in the body have different amino acid sequences, they are nevertheless similar in structure. The electrophoresis technique permits the separation of proteins so that certain ones that scientists want to study can be separated from all the others.

In the late 1940s scientists began finding multiple forms of the same protein in people's blood, fluids, and tissues. Other animals and plants showed similar protein variations. These stable, inherited variations in protein structure reflect differences in DNA. At the time biologists did not have good methods to study DNA directly, but methods for studying proteins were rapidly evolving. One was electrophoresis, a separation technique. Another related technique is called isoelectric focusing, and it was in some ways superior to electrophoresis for separating and analyzing protein mixtures. At the same time advances in immunology and in enzymology made the detection of specific proteins possible.

Immunological techniques make use of antibodies. Antibodies to almost any protein can be made by injecting a solution of that protein into an animal (usually a rabbit or a goat), waiting until the animal forms antibodies to the protein in its blood, then collecting the blood and using the watery portion (the serum) as an antibody solution. For example, antibodies to a serum protein called GC (group-specific component) could be produced in a rabbit in this way. The antibodies could then be used to detect GC specifically in a sample of someone's blood serum that has undergone electrophoresis to separate out the proteins. Scientists did this sort of work extensively and found that many of the blood proteins showed polymorphism—there were several different, genetically

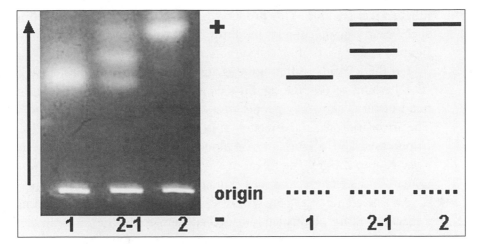

Typing isoenzymes by the zymogram method, illustrated by a red cell isoenzyme called esterase D. At left is an image of an actual gel that was run and stained. At right is a diagrammatic representation of the esterase D isoenzyme patterns for the common genetic types. Before DNA technology was developed, forensic scientists used variations in isoenzyme type proteins to help narrow down who might be the source of a blood or other body fluid specimen. *(Courtesy of the author)*

determined forms of them in different people. These were called serum protein polymorphisms, and forensic scientists moved quickly to use them to help individualize dried blood.

The main serum protein polymorphisms used in forensic science were GC, haptoglobin (HP), and transferrin (TF). These polymorphic serum proteins are not enzymes. As a result they usually have to be detected with specific antibodies made in an animal or by using some intrinsic property of the protein itself. For example, haptoglobin is the hemoglobin-binding protein of human serum: It binds to free hemoglobin (hemoglobin that is outside red cells) and transports it to the liver for metabolic processing. One can take advantage of haptoglobin's hemoglobin-binding property to make it visible on an electrophoresis gel.

There are many enzymes in blood as well, many of them within the red cells. And it turned out that quite a few of them showed multiple molecular forms; that is, different people would have different but stable forms of the same enzyme. Such forms were called isoenzymes. As noted earlier, enzymes are biological catalysts—they specifically speed up a biochemical reaction. This property is useful as a means of detecting specific enzymes in complex mixtures. The procedure, illustrated in the figure on page 35, is often called the zymogram technique.

On the left side of the figure is an image of part of an esterase D (ESD) typing gel. On the right is a diagrammatic representation of the band patterns shown by people who are type 1, type 2-1, and type 2. The arrow indicates the direction of isoenzyme migration during electrophoresis. The "origin" is where bloodstained thread specimens were inserted into the gel. The threads glow because the gel is being viewed under ultraviolet light, and they contain a "brightener."

An isoenzyme typing analysis of a bloodstain was done by inserting a specimen of the bloodstain into a gel and subjecting the gel to electrophoresis. All of the proteins in the blood were present in that specimen, and they would move in the gel in response to the electrophoresis. When the electrophoresis is stopped, the different proteins are spread out over the different parts of the gel. The analyst is interested in visualizing only one specific enzyme, and that is what the zymogram technique does. The chemicals that participate in the enzyme's normal reaction are added. The enzyme will speed up the chemical reaction and form the usual products. The analyst then looks for the reaction product. Wherever there is reaction product, there must have been the enzyme of interest. In the end the only thing visible is the product of the enzyme reaction, and it is located right where the enzyme is. Each of the different molecular forms of the enzyme catalyzes the reaction just as well, so there is a pattern on the gel representing the isoenzyme type.

The more scientists studied the proteins of blood and tissues, the more variation they found. Polymorphism is common rather than rare. Of course, that finding turned out to be useful for forensic scientists. They want to use these differences to try to narrow down whom a blood or body fluid specimen might have come from. As shown in the sidebar "Using Isoenzyme Types to Include and Exclude Bloodstain Sources," the way this is actually done depends on genetics, in particular on the branch called population genetics.

For most of the 1970s and 1980s forensic scientists used isoenzyme and serum protein types in addition to ABO blood types for this purpose. Under favorable conditions—that is, conditions where bloodstains had not been too damaged by exposure to the environment—quite a few genetic systems could be typed in dried blood. In body fluids the variety that could be typed was much more limited, mostly just to one isoenzyme called PGM. The reason was that many of the isoenzymes and serum proteins that can be detected in blood are not present in body fluids. This situation illustrates an important feature about human genetics: A gene can be expressed (can actively make its protein product) in one tissue but be "turned off" in other tissues.

An additional example of the extent of human genetic variation, the HLA system, deserves mention. HLA stands for human leukocyte antigen. It is a complex set of tissue antigens, and a person's HLA antigen profile is highly individual. These antigens also occur on white blood cells. Lymphocytes, one of the white blood cell types, were traditionally used for HLA typing. The genetic region responsible for these antigens is called the histocompatibility locus region. These antigens are responsible in large part for compatibility or rejection in tissue or organ transplants. HLA typing was used for parentage testing for quite some time, but it never worked for bloodstains.

All the blood type, isoenzyme, and serum protein polymorphisms that forensic scientists relied on for many decades have now been replaced. Once it became possible to work directly with DNA and to look at human polymorphism and variation in that way, the blood types and proteins were no longer needed. DNA typing is much more powerful in its ability to tell people apart than were the traditional systems. It is now possible to individualize (for all practical purposes) biological specimens. There have already been several iterations of DNA technology, each new one replacing the former. All of these methods have been made possible by advances in the study of genetics.

THE OLD DAYS TO NOWADAYS: MILESTONES IN GENETICS

Forensic testing that can effectively individualize biological evidence— that is, show that it came from a particular person—is based on the principles underlying DNA and the principles underlying genetics. The earliest geneticists studied inheritance in individual families of organisms back in the 19th century. Later scientists developed the principles of population genetics.

Using Isoenzyme Types to Include and Exclude Bloodstain Sources

In a suburban community near a large city a woman was violently assaulted in her home. She had arrived home and surprised a burglar. She fought with the intruder briefly and received injuries, from blows and from being cut with a knife. She did not get a very good look at the perpetrator. There had been a series of burglaries in the area, and police had some information from other victims that eventually led them to charge a man with the burglaries and with the assault on this woman.

Police obtained a warrant to search the suspect's residence for clothes that might have some blood on them from the struggle with the assault victim. They seized a pair of trousers that appeared to be bloodstained. The trousers, along with blood standards from the suspect and the assault victim, were submitted to the forensic laboratory for examination. The stains on the trousers were of human blood, and the genetic typing results were as shown in the following table.

	ABO	PGM	ESD	GLO	ACP	AK	ADA
Assault victim	A	2+1+	1	2-1	BA	1	1
Suspect	O	2+1+	1	2-1	B	1	2-1
Trouser stains	A	2+1+	1	2-1	BA	1	1

The first column of results is the ABO type of the people and the evidence. The rest of the columns are isoenzyme name abbreviations. Each abbreviation has a specific meaning and a set of characteristics associated with it. But it is not necessary for one to understand all the numbers and letters to understand this case. One can look through the table and quickly see what matches and what does not. The genetic systems are independent, so a nonmatch in any column would be an exclusion.

What the table shows is that the stains on the trousers are not of the suspect's blood. This fact is clear from the ABO type: He is O, and the stain is A. The stains came from someone else. They could be from the assault victim, because all the system types match. But that does not mean the stains came from her to the exclusion of all other people; this kind of blood analysis is not powerful enough to individualize. So, what can be said or concluded by the analyst?

Here is where population genetics comes into this picture. Population genetics is a big subject, but briefly, scientists can find out how often each different type in each of the systems is seen by typing people in the population for all the genetic systems. These numbers give pretty good estimates of the actual distributions. They are estimates because it is not practical to type everyone; a sample of people is typed. The other important factor is that all these systems are inherited independently; that is, the ABO type that someone inherits from his or her parents does not influence nor is it influenced by the PGM type he or she inherits, and so on. This is like successive flips of a coin, or successive throws of dice. What one gets on the first toss is independent of what one might get on the second toss.

What it all means is that one can multiply the separate occurrences (or probabilities) together to get the combined figure. For instance, the chances of a head on the first coin toss are ½ (or 50 percent). The chances of getting two heads in a row are ½ times ½ (or 25 percent). The chances of getting three heads in a row are ½ times ½ times ½ (or 12.5 percent), and so forth.

The same thing can be done with the data in the table above. It is possible to figure out about how many people in the population would have all the types found on the trouser stains. This figure comes out to about 2 percent for Caucasians (the number would be different if the calculation were done for African Americans, Hispanics, Asians, or another group). So the analyst could tell the court that, if the blood came from a Caucasian, it could have come from about two in every 100 people. In other words, it could have come from the victim in the case, but it could also have come from many other people. In a city of 1 million people, 20,000 would be expected to have the set of types seen in this evidence.

The case shows how several genetic systems can be used together to decrease the size of the population segment that a specimen might have come from. It also shows that even if one gets results that yield a fairly low percentage of the population as possible depositors, there are still quite a few people who share the same types.

Gregor Mendel is considered the father of classical genetics. *(Mendel Center at the Abbey of St. Thomas, Brno, Czech Republic)*

Gregor Mendel: Inheritance Among the Pea Plants

The earliest known systematic experiments in genetics were performed by an Augustinian monk named Gregor Mendel (1823–84). Although his work was presented and recorded in a scientific proceeding in 1865, not many people heard about it until more than three decades later. The scientific society and its proceedings, where the work was originally described, were obscure, and no one in mainstream science at the time saw it or paid attention.

Working in the garden of a monastery in Brünn, Austria (modern-day Brno, Czech Republic), Mendel performed carefully controlled experiments on inheritance in common garden pea plants. Mendel studied seven characteristics of the pea plants, including red versus white flower color, tall versus short, and smooth versus wrinkled seed texture.

By crossing plants with known characteristics in controlled breeding experiments and recording the numbers of offspring that had each of the characteristics, Mendel was able to infer how the characteristics were being inherited. He proposed the concept of the gene as the unit of inheritance of these characteristics, and he hypothesized that each individual has a pair of genes for each characteristic, one inherited at random from each parent. His fundamental discoveries are now often

Monastery garden in Brno, Czech Republic, as it looks today. Gregor Mendel's work was done in a greenhouse that once stood in this area. *(Courtesy of the author)*

known as Mendel's laws, and simple inheritance patterns in families are sometimes called "Mendelian."

Molecular Genetics: The Fruit Fly, Bread Mold, and Bacteria Pioneers

Around 1900 the study of genetics really took off. One pioneering group was that of the noted biologist Thomas Hunt Morgan, a faculty member of Columbia University in New York City. Around this time the fruit fly, *Drosophila melanogaster*, became the geneticist's research animal of choice. These little flies have many characteristics that are easy to observe under a magnifier or a low-power microscope and that are inherited in simple ways. Fruit flies are fairly easy to maintain in the laboratory, have short reproductive cycles, and produce many offspring. These features are ideal for doing genetic research.

Morgan attracted some very gifted students—A. H. Sturtevant, Calvin Bridges, and H. J. Muller—who would go on to become first-rate geneticists. Morgan was awarded the Nobel Prize in 1933, and Muller received it in 1946, for discoveries in genetics. Along with others these pioneers established the physical basis for inheritance: Genes are carried in structures called chromosomes, of which humans have 46. They confirmed and extended Mendel's basic rules and also found a number of new genetic phenomena, including the process of crossing over, how mutations can be induced, and the mechanism of sex-linked inheritance.

Molecular genetics is the study of the molecular mechanisms within DNA and RNA that explain the underlying basis of inheritance. One could argue that the era of biochemical genetics, or molecular genetics, began with the studies of George Beadle and E. L. Tatum using the bread mold *Neurospora crassa* as a research organism beginning in 1941. They were interested in establishing that a gene (within the DNA) was responsible for a specific protein or enzyme, a concept known as the "one gene—one enzyme" hypothesis. The methods to do that kind of detailed biochemical work in the fruit fly were not available at the time, so Beadle and Tatum chose bread mold.

Bread mold has several useful features for genetic research. It can be grown in simple, laboratory-prepared media in petri dishes. Mutations can be induced in the mold that change its nutritional requirements in simple, straightforward ways. This information can then be used to figure out that a gene controlling a particular enzyme in a nutritional pathway has been altered. Their work allowed them to formulate the one gene–one enzyme hypothesis, and in 1958 they, along with Joshua Lederberg, were awarded the Nobel Prize for their discoveries in molecular genetics.

Finally, one of the most famous experiments in the history of biology was conducted by Oswald T. Avery, Colin M. MacLeod, and Maclyn McCarty. In 1944 they showed conclusively that deoxyribonucleic acid, or DNA, is the genetic material. Their cleverly designed protocol, described in the sidebar "DNA Is the Genetic Material," involved infection of bacterial cells by a virus that normally infected them.

How DNA Regulates Cell Activity: Controlling the Synthesis of Proteins

As the Avery-MacLeod-McCarty experiments in the 1940s showed, DNA specifies the cell's activities. It was now clear that DNA directs the course of cell development and differentiation in multicellular animals, thus forming the individual. It then has a role in maintaining life functions, in repair of damaged cells or tissues, in healing, and in fighting off disease. But scientists did not yet understand how DNA accomplished these activities. Its pivotal role in specifying the sequence of amino acids in proteins was established in the 1960s.

During the decade biochemical methods improved, making it easier to figure out how genes actually worked. The structure of DNA had been established in 1953 by James Watson and Francis Crick, and scientists began unraveling how DNA uses ribonucleic acid, or RNA, to specify the synthesis of proteins. Robert Holley, H. G. Khorana, and Marshall Nirenberg shared the Nobel Prize in 1968 for their key roles in describing this process. They discovered that DNA specifies the structure of RNA and that RNA in turn specifies the structure of protein. DNA works through RNA in specifying protein structure. It does this by way of the genetic code. Three DNA bases in a row specify, through intermediary RNA, a building block of a protein called an amino acid.

The process by which DNA functions to tell the cell how to make its proteins has been called the "central dogma of molecular biology." Since many proteins are enzymes, whose presence or absence determines whether a certain reaction can occur or not, specification of protein structure is one important way DNA regulates cell activity.

DNA Is the Genetic Material

In 1944 Oswald T. Avery, Colin M. MacLeod, and Maclyn McCarty of the Rockefeller Institute in New York published a paper in the *Journal of Experimental Medicine* that was to become a classic. Scientists had suspected for some time that DNA was the genetic material, but it had not been experimentally established unequivocally. The question was, Is it really DNA that carries information from one generation to the next?

There are two forms of the pneumococcus bacterium, called R and S. R is a nonencapsulated and nonvirulent form, while S is an encapsulated, virulent (infectious) form. It was known that the R form could be transformed into the S form in an animal by injecting a heat-killed preparation of S and a small quantity of living R. Somehow the R form that does not cause disease was being transformed into the S form that causes pneumonia. Avery, MacLeod, and McCarty wanted to find out the nature of the "transforming" principle. Was it DNA, or was it protein? The question is not as simple as it sounds, because DNA in the nucleus of cells has some proteins associated with it.

They purified the "transforming" principle, the chemical material that they could show was bringing about the R to S transformation, and tested it using a number of methods to help characterize its nature. The methods included chemical analysis, enzyme digestion, and serological reactions. Chemical analysis indicated that the material was consistent with the known composition of DNA but not of protein. Using different enzymes to digest the material (in order to try to destroy the transforming activity), the researchers showed that enzymes that disrupt DNA disrupted the transforming activity. Finally, the serological reaction testing showed that the cell's non-nuclear material was not involved in the transformation.

The results of the experiments showed convincingly that DNA was responsible for determining whether the cell was R or S. The DNA was dictating the cell type and thus its disease-causing ability. Thus, DNA was the genetic material, the material that controlled cell function. By extension DNA was thus the material that carries the information for dictating cell function from generation to generation, because DNA is what passes from generation to generation. Many other experiments by many scientists have confirmed these findings.

The Genome Project and DNA Polymorphism (Variation)

One of the most impressive feats in the history of biology has been the complete sequencing of human DNA. The DNA of a number of other species has now been fully sequenced as well. Certain advancements in technology that made high-throughput (high-capacity) sequencing possible and practical helped to speed the process along. Advancements in a field called bioinformatics, which keeps track of huge amounts of very similar data in an organized way, were also part of the solution. Even with all that it took several years to complete the first sequence.

In chapter 3 the structure of DNA will be discussed in more detail. For now think of DNA as being made up of a four-letter alphabet. The letters are A, T, C, and G, and it is the order in which they occur in DNA in a long, long sequence string (around 3 billion letters) that makes up the DNA "sequence." These letters represent biochemical units called bases. The first complete human sequences were published in scientific journals in 2001. Two groups, a private group led by Craig Venter at Celera and a government group led by Francis Collins, independently worked out the first sequences.

The completed sequence held a few surprises. For one there is a very large amount of repeat sequence DNA in the genome (the total DNA in one regular cell). Some of the repeats are fairly long, while others are fairly short. The shortest repeated unit is two letters. Much of the repeat-sequence DNA is scattered around in the genome, but some of it is arranged linearly in a head-to-tail, or tandem, fashion.

Forensic scientists are especially interested in this kind of "tandemly repeated" sequence DNA. It turns out that there is considerable variation among people as to how many repeats one finds at a given location in DNA, or to put it another way, there is considerable polymorphism at many of the tandem-repeat sequence locations. If methods could be devised to measure the different numbers of repeats, people could be told apart using these polymorphic features of DNA. And, that is exactly what forensic scientists have done.

NOWADAYS: THE DNA ERA

Much of the repeated sequence data in the human genome is not functional; it does not specify protein structure. It has been called "junk DNA," though it may have functions that are not yet clear to scientists. About 20 percent of human DNA is functional, in the sense that it codes for protein. And, within that 20 percent, there is considerable similarity in sequence among different people. This is exactly what would be expected; the structure of functional DNA would be conserved. Any major alterations in the sequence of the functional DNA would lead to problems with the specification of protein structure and would likely cause problems for the individual.

Changes in one or a few bases in DNA are called mutations, and they do occur. Study of variations in functional proteins, such as hemoglobin, makes it clear that some mutations are innocuous. Scientists know this because these mutated versions of hemoglobin are found in living people. In other words, there has been a mutation in DNA, and it has caused a change in the hemoglobin protein, but the person with the mutation is alive and well. The mutation did not therefore affect the functionality of the hemoglobin. But many mutations do cause problems with protein functionality. These problems often lead to serious medical problems. Many mutations probably lead to early death—so early in the development of an embryo that the mother may not yet even realize she is pregnant. Scientists will never see the mutations that prevent such an embryo from surviving.

In the 80 percent or so of DNA that does not specify protein structure, there is enormous sequence and repeat-sequence polymorphism. For the most part it does not seem to have any negative consequences for the individual and can be exploited for purposes of identification, as has been done by forensic scientists.

Sir Alec Jeffreys: DNA Analysis Meets Forensic Science

In the 1980s DNA scientists (molecular geneticists) focused on the repeat-sequence polymorphism within DNA. For most researchers these repeat-sequence regions were "road signs" along the sequence of letters (bases) as different laboratories worked on sequencing the entire human DNA. Dr. Alec Jeffreys at the University of Leicester in the United Kingdom realized that these polymorphisms provided excellent tools for human identification in affiliation cases, especially when many regions were examined simultaneously. He called these patterns "DNA fingerprints," a term that has stuck, especially in the popular media. Most forensic scientists dislike the term because it can create confusion between DNA and conventional fingerprints, and because there are some differences between DNA individuality and fingerprint individuality. Jeffreys published several papers on this subject in the prestigious scientific journal *Nature* in 1985.

Around this same time, in 1983 and in 1986, two teenage girls had been raped and murdered in the small village of Narborough in Leicestershire, England (see sidebar "The Narborough Murders"). Jeffreys and DNA technology would be drawn into this case, and its outcome became the flash point for the development of DNA-typing methods in forensic science laboratories worldwide.

Within a couple of years forensic science laboratories all over the world had acquired the tools to perform the new DNA-typing technique. Jeffreys's name will be forever linked with this revolution. In 1998, at its 50th anniversary meeting in San Francisco, the American Academy of Forensic Sciences paid special tribute to Jeffreys in recognition of his contributions.

Development of Forensic DNA Typing

Starting in the 1980s, methods were developed that made DNA sequencing much easier and faster than it had been. These methods could be automated, enabling a very large amount of sequence data to be collected in many laboratories throughout the world. With these methodologies in place in the larger research centers, the U.S. government and a private company made commitments to pursue sequencing the entire human genome. This task, one of the more impressive in the history of biological science, was completed in the late 1990s.

As sequence data accumulated it became clear that a large fraction of human DNA was not involved in specifying protein structure; that is, it did not seem to have any obvious function. It has been called "junk DNA" for this reason. Much, but not all, of this nonfunctional DNA has repetitive sequences. There are several different types of repeat-sequence DNA, but the most important for purposes of human identification, and thus forensic purposes, is a kind that has head-to-tail sequences repeated one after the other along the DNA strand. Many regions in the human DNA have this type of repeated sequence structure, known as tandem repeats. The reason tandem-repeated DNA is useful for human identification is that there is a lot of variation among different people in the number of times the sequence is repeated.

Jeffreys was studying regions of DNA that have the head-to-tail repeat sequences when he developed the first forensic DNA typing. Under certain lab conditions many of these regions can be examined simultaneously using a technique called restriction fragment length polymorphism (RFLP). RFLP will be fully described in chapter 3, but briefly, the technique generates a series of parallel light and dark lines on X-ray film. It looks something like a bar code. Every individual has a different DNA "bar code," and this observation forms the basis of forensic DNA typing—that is, DNA typing for human identification.

Since the 1980s, when the earliest versions of forensic DNA typing were developed, several new technologies have been developed and

The Narborough Murders

In 1983, in England, a 15-year-old girl who was walking home along a country lane near Enderby became the victim of rape and murder. The investigation yielded no suspects. Three years later another young girl was sexually assaulted and murdered in a similar manner in the nearby village of Narborough. Police arrested a teenager named Rodney Buckland, who worked in a local mental hospital. Buckland had made statements incriminating himself in the second murder but proclaiming his innocence in the earlier one.

The police were certain that Buckland had raped and killed both girls. They sent semen samples recovered from the two victims, along with a blood sample from Buckland, to Alec Jeffreys for examination using his new DNA-typing method. The DNA analysis confirmed that the same offender had committed both crimes as police suspected, but it showed that Buckland was excluded. His incriminating statements were false. Thus, Buckland became the first man ever exonerated by DNA typing. Without it he might well have gone to jail for a very long time.

The police then began a massive manhunt for the true perpetrator. They conducted what might be called a "biological evidence dragnet," or "DNA dragnet." All the males in the village between the ages of about 14 and 70 were requested to provide reference blood specimens. Most

implemented. The most important breakthrough was using a technique called polymerase chain reaction (PCR) to make multiple copies of small quantities of DNA in a specimen for subsequent typing.

The Polymerase Chain Reaction

The original DNA-typing method, the one Jeffreys used in the Narborough case, was too cumbersome and time consuming to be useful for casework and database construction. A different, faster technology was needed. It was developed in 1985.

The polymerase chain reaction is one of the most stunning breakthroughs in all DNA science. The idea is attributable to Kary Mullis, who

did so—more than 5,000 in all. At this point DNA typing was very new; forensic science laboratories did not even perform it yet. Jeffreys had agreed to do the DNA typing in his lab at the University of Leicester. Because this early form of DNA typing was very complex and time consuming, the Home Office (U.K. government) forensic science lab first "screened" all the specimens using the conventional genetic-marker systems that were discussed earlier in this chapter. This excluded most of the men as potential semen donors on the basis of their ABO blood types, secretor status, and/or isoenzyme types, and they were thus excluded from further consideration as suspects. The remaining specimens were then sent for DNA typing.

In the first round of DNA typing none of the men's samples matched the types of the semen donor in the crimes. The perpetrator, a 27-year-old named Colin Pitchfork, was ultimately found, arrested, and convicted of the offenses, because he had paid someone to give police a voluntary blood specimen using his name. He bragged about this ruse while drinking in a pub, was overheard, and was turned in to the police. The surrogate, when confronted, admitted to the police what he had done. Pitchfork's DNA types matched those found in the semen recovered from both victims.

worked for Cetus Corporation at the time; he received the Nobel Prize in chemistry in 1993 for his discovery. Cetus scientists commercialized PCR, and it has been extensively used in research and application laboratories, including forensic science labs, all over the world.

Essentially, PCR copies a segment of DNA multiple times using an enzyme called a DNA polymerase. The segment that is to be copied is specified, or defined, by two primers. In this way a small amount of DNA can be used to make a very large number of copies of a desired small portion of the total molecule. This process has been extremely useful in basic and applied biomedical research and as the basis for clinical and forensic tests. There have been two generations of forensic DNA tests based on the PCR, and they are discussed in chapter 3.

Forensic DNA typing is based on a simple principle: A person's DNA type is a statement about how many times the head-to-tail repeat sequences are repeated. Chromosomes are paired, and on these pairs one chromosome has a repeat number inherited from the mother, while on the other chromosome is a repeat number inherited from the father. In the majority of people the numbers are different. Combining information about these numbers of repeats at several regions in the DNA can generate a profile that is very unlikely to be found in more than a single individual.

3

DNA and Genetics

Understanding forensic DNA analysis requires some understanding of both genetics and the structure and functions of DNA. The basic principles of genetics and of population genetics apply to DNA. The entire DNA of a person, contained in 46 structures within the nucleus called chromosomes, constitutes what is called the human genome. The task of DNA is to regulate cell function. DNA regulates cell function indirectly, by specifying protein structure. Any change in DNA that leads to a change in protein structure will likely affect cell function. The task of the chromosomes, in turn, is to transport the DNA from cell to cell and from generation to generation. When sperm and eggs are made, it is the chromosomes that are replicated and then apportioned.

DNA is at the core of inheritance, and the fact that DNA is inherited according to simple rules makes it possible to use DNA typing as a forensic tool. DNA typing can thus be used to individualize blood and physiological fluids, to identify human remains, and to include or exclude persons in disputed parentage cases.

BASIC PRINCIPLES OF INHERITANCE

As discussed briefly in chapter 2, the fundamental principles of inheritance on which the science of genetics is based were first discovered by Gregor Mendel. Mendel's laws specify two basic principles of inheritance: segregation and independent assortment.

The first law, segregation, says that a pair of genes separate when germ cells (sperm or egg) are formed, and each germ cell gets one gene or the other. Today it is understood that this law derives from the process of meiosis (see figure). In ordinary cell division the chromosomes (and the DNA they contain) are replicated, then apportioned equally between the daughter cells. This process, also illustrated in the figure, is called mitosis.

But in meiosis, after the chromosomes (and DNA) are replicated they undergo two rounds of cell division. The first is equivalent to mitosis: Each daughter cell has one copy of all the chromosomes. But in the next division the chromosome pairs (and all the genes in the DNA of the chromosome pairs) separate. As a result one daughter cell gets one member of the chromosome pair (and half the DNA), and the other daughter cell gets the other chromosome (and the other half of the DNA). The resulting germ cells (sperm or egg cells) have half the number of chromosomes and half the DNA of the original cell. The original number of chromosomes is restored when a sperm cell fertilizes an egg.

A gene is a functional unit within DNA that consists of all of the DNA necessary to specify the structure of a whole protein or a whole subunit of a protein. A gene is therefore a long sequence of DNA within a chromosome. Humans have 46 chromosomes in all their cells except gametes (sperm or egg). Forty-four of them are paired with a homologous (physically and functionally similar) partner; the other two are sex chromosomes. The sex chromosomes are either X or Y. Females have two Xs. Males have an X and a Y. When a female makes egg cells, each one has 23 chromosomes, one of which is X. When a male makes sperm cells, each one also has 23 chromosomes, but half the sperm will have an X and half will have a Y.

The genes controlling a particular trait are at a particular location on the chromosome. This location is called a locus (from the Latin word for "place"; the plural is *loci*). Because there is a pair of chromosomes, there is a pair of genes. The pair of genes at the same locus of homologous

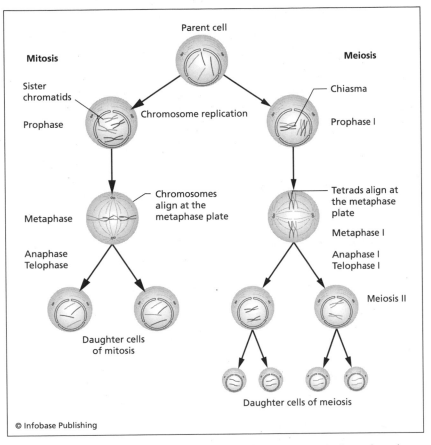

Meiosis and mitosis: On the right is reduction division, or meiosis, and on the left is normal cell division, or mitosis. Note that mitosis yields daughter cells with chromosone number identical to that of the parent, while meiosis yields daughter cells with chromosome number half that of the parent.

chromosomes is called "alleles." At any given point on the chromosome, the gene pair (the alleles) might be the same on both chromosomes, or they might be different. If the alleles are the same, the person is said to be homozygous at the locus; if the alleles are different, the person is heterozygous.

The same terms are used even if the DNA does not have a known function. For example, there is a repeated sequence location (locus) on chromosome 18 that is used in forensic DNA analysis. The number of repeats on a chromosome varies in different people from about 11 to 22.

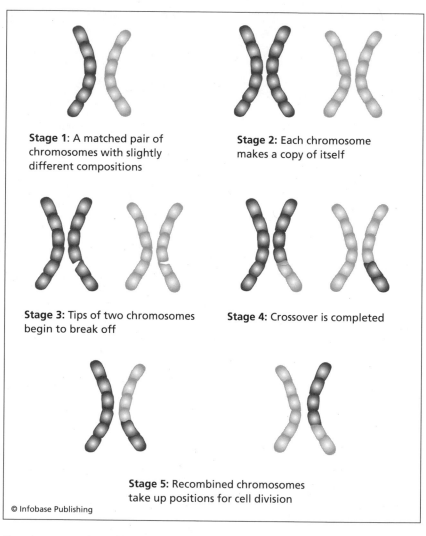

Stage 1: A matched pair of chromosomes with slightly different compositions

Stage 2: Each chromosome makes a copy of itself

Stage 3: Tips of two chromosomes begin to break off

Stage 4: Crossover is completed

Stage 5: Recombined chromosomes take up positions for cell division

© Infobase Publishing

Crossing over. Also called recombination, this process results in chromosomes in daughter cells that are different from either of those in the parent cell resulting in greater genetic variability in offspring.

If a person had 11 repeats at the locus on both chromosomes, one would say he or she was homozygous at the locus; if the number of repeats on the chromosomes was different on each chromosome, the person would be referred to as heterozygous.

Mendel's second law says that the simultaneous inheritance of two characteristics is determined independently. This is called the law of independent assortment. It is now known that this principle applies to gene loci on different chromosomes. The chromosomes are indeed inherited independently. Inheritance is somewhat more complicated than what is represented by Mendel's basic rules, however. During meiosis the replicated chromosomes, which are lined up next to one another, can physically exchange chromosomal material. This phenomenon is called "crossing over," or genetic recombination (see figure). (There are other complexities in genetics and inheritance as well, but they are not important to understanding forensic DNA analysis.)

During meiosis, when the chromosomes are lined up during replication, they can physically exchange homologous (corresponding) pieces. This crossing-over process provides another source of genetic diversity. The recombination leads to combinations of genes on different parts of the same chromosome that would not be possible without it. The result is that more genetic diversity is created in the species over time. In the figure, the chromosomes resulting from crossing-over are different from either member of the chromosome pair in the parent cell.

STRUCTURE AND FUNCTION OF DNA

Biological scientists have known about DNA for quite a while, but they did not know the structure until 1953. In that year James Watson and Francis Crick proposed the now classical double helix, based in large part on X-ray diffraction data. They, along with Maurice Wilkins, were awarded the Nobel Prize in physiology or medicine in 1962 for these discoveries.

As shown in the figure, each strand consists of a deoxyribose sugar-phosphate (D-P) backbone. The strands are held together by hydrogen bonds, weak chemical bonds linking H and O atoms, between the bases. Each D-P component has a base chemically associated with it. There are four bases in DNA: adenine (A), thymine (T), cytosine (C), and guanine (G). The bases on one strand pair with the bases on the other strand by hydrogen bonding. A always pairs with T, and C always pairs with G. If one strand has an A, the other will have a T at that location; similarly, if one strand has a C, the other will have a G at the location. Two hydrogen

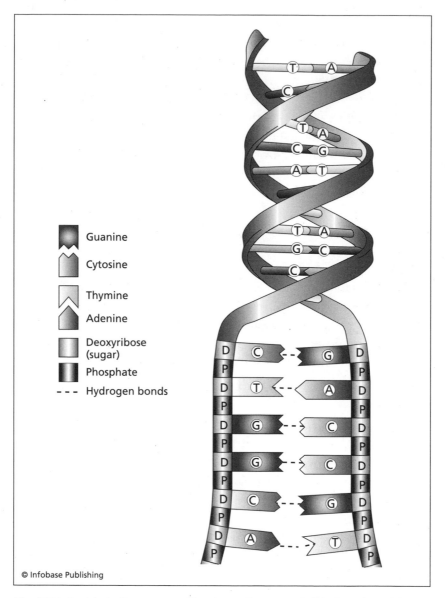

Guanine

Cytosine

Thymine

Adenine

Deoxyribose (sugar)

Phosphate

- - - Hydrogen bonds

© Infobase Publishing

The DNA double-helix structure. The deoxyribose sugar (D)-phosphate (P) backbone of the helical structure is visible along with the T-A and C-G pairs that form the "rungs of the ladder."

bonds form between A and T, while three can form between G and C. The force holding G-C together is thus a little greater than that holding A-T. Each hydrogen bond is quite weak, but there are thousands and thousands of nucleotides in DNA, and the sum of all the weak hydrogen bonds holds the double-stranded molecule together.

The strands are twisted around each other to form the double helix. Each strand is made up of what biochemists call nucleotides. One nucleotide consists of a deoxyribose sugar (D), a phosphate (P), and a base (A, T, C, or G). One DNA strand is a polymer of nucleotides, a long chain of these smaller molecules bonded together.

Sorting out DNA function was the essence of molecular biology in the 1960s and early 1970s. The bottom line is that DNA specifies the structure of proteins. Just how it does so has turned out to be rather complicated. DNA molecules differ from one another by the sequence of the bases. But DNA is a huge molecule, and the number of different ways one can arrange the sequence of the four bases is enormous. The sequence of the bases is what determines protein structure.

Proteins are molecules made up of amino acids bonded together. Just as DNA is a polymer of nucleotides, a protein is a polymer of amino acids. There are about 20 different amino acids that can occur in proteins. The sequence of bases in DNA that specifies the sequence of amino acids in proteins is called the "genetic code." Three bases in the DNA sequence constitute a "word," that is, the triplet (also known as a codon) that specifies a certain amino acid. DNA in fact controls protein synthesis by way of another nucleic acid called ribonucleic acid, or RNA. Unlike DNA, RNA consists of a single strand of nucleotides. Another difference is that where DNA has the base thymine (T), RNA has the base uracil (U).

To make a specific protein the cell uses one of the DNA strands to make an RNA strand of complementary sequence. This RNA is called messenger RNA, or mRNA. *Complementary sequence* means that each nucleotide of the m-RNA contains, not the same base as that in DNA, but the one that pairs with it; for example, the DNA sequence ACGTTC would make mRNA with the sequence UGCAAG (remember that RNA has U instead of T). This process is known as transcription. After transcription the mRNA strand can be "translated" to a protein. Protein synthesis also involves another RNA molecule called transfer RNA, or tRNA, which serves as an "adaptor" molecule. Transfer RNA is hairpin shaped. One end has a three-base sequence, an anticodon, that is complementary to the codon in mRNA, while the other end can bind a particular amino acid.

The figure shows the process of translation. The genetic code word AUC, shown in the figure, is said to "code for" the amino acid isoleucine. That means that the sequence AUC in mRNA will attract isoleucine tRNA because isoleucine tRNA has the UAG anticodon; UAG is the complement of AUC. The mRNA triplet AUC is shown binding its anticodon UAG, but the amino acid isoleucine is not identified. It is shown as a dot. The next two codons in the figure, CGU and UCG, code for the amino acids arginine and serine, respectively. So the three dots representing the growing protein (at step 6) would be isoleucine-arginine-serine. This translation process takes place in the ribosomes, which are small organelles within the cell, and specific enzymes are involved in both the transcription and translation steps. This flow of information, from DNA to mRNA to protein, is often called the central dogma of molecular biology.

Another important feature of DNA is the ability to self-replicate and to do so accurately. Everyone starts out as one cell, yet each person ends up as billions of cells, each of which has an identical copy of DNA in its nucleus. For that to be possible DNA must be able to copy itself accurately. DNA must replicate each time a cell divides so that the daughter cells will have identical copies. The DNA replication process is catalyzed by special enzymes called DNA polymerases. Certain DNA polymerases have a role to play in forensic DNA typing, and this topic will be discussed later in this chapter.

Structural Variation in DNA among Different People

It is often remarked that no two people except identical twins have the same DNA. As far as scientists now know, the statement is true, but like many generalizations, it hides a lot of the detail. What the human genome project has shown is that about 20 percent of human DNA actually specifies protein structure. Much of the DNA that specifies protein structure is pretty similar among different people. The differences that do exist—polymorphism in DNA—cause protein and enzyme polymorphism.

Polymorphism in DNA is simply a base change here or there from one person to another. A single base change in coding DNA might cause a different amino acid to be inserted into the protein; but some single-base changes would not even do that, because several triplet sequences

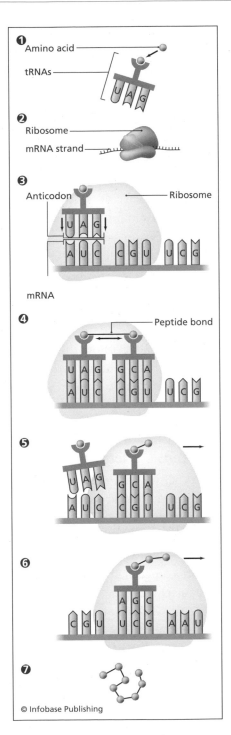

❶ Amino acid

tRNAs

❷ Ribosome

mRNA strand

❸ Anticodon · · · · · · · · · · · · Ribosome

mRNA

❹ Peptide bond

❺

❻

❼

© Infobase Publishing

Protein synthesis: How DNA specifies protein structure. Transfer RNA (tRNA) molecules associate with a single amino acid (1). The other end of the tRNA molecule contains a specific three-base sequence that is complementary to a three-base sequence in mRNA (3). The mRNA sequence is complementary to the coding strand of DNA (not shown in this picture). With the help of a cellular structure called a ribosome (2), the tRNA molecules lock onto the complementary sequences of mRNA, and thus line up the amino acids (4), which can then be covalently linked together by an enzyme to form a peptide bond, thus beginning the synthesis of a protein (5, 6, 7).

of the genetic code can specify the same amino acid. As long as the base changes do not cause too great a change in the protein structure, the protein is still functional. These single-base changes in DNA over time become mutations, and they occur in all cells. Mutations that cause major disruption in the structure (and thus function) of vital proteins generally do not allow the organism that has them to survive, meaning that the mutation does not survive either. But many mutations do survive and create the polymorphism in DNA and proteins that is so common.

In spite of many single-base differences throughout the genome, there is considerable similarity in the DNA of most people. It is not realistic right now to sequence large segments of DNA just to find the differences between people because the process would be too burdensome. The Human Genome Project has provided considerable information about where the differences are, however, and technology is rapidly being developed that will allow searches for hundreds or thousands of small differences all at once.

There is another kind of variation in DNA, however, that has been exploited for forensic DNA typing. As already noted, about 20 percent of human DNA specifies protein structure. What about the remaining 80 percent? What does it do? No one is sure, but there is something very interesting about much of this remaining "nonfunctional" DNA: It has a lot of repeated sequences.

The DNA Variation of Interest to Forensic Scientists

As discussed earlier, the regions of DNA that forensic scientists use to individualize people contain repeated sequences. There are different types of repeat-sequence DNA. A repeated sequence may be found in many different places in the genome. These can be called "interspersed" sequences. Some repeated sequences are head-to-tail repeats of a sequence altogether at one location within the DNA. These are sometimes called "tandem" repeats, and they are the ones that forensic scientists use.

In the context of these regions of DNA the variation between people consists of the number of repeats at a tandem-repeat location. One person might have 10 repeats, and someone else might have 12 or 14 or some other number. The physical structures that contains the DNA are the chromosomes, and humans have 46 chromosomes, which are grouped into 23 pairs. One member of each pair is inherited from one's mother,

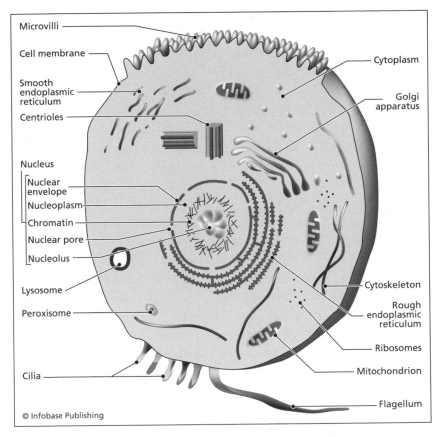

A generalized animal cell that shows nucleus and mitochondria. Not every animal has all the parts shown in the figure.

and the other comes from one's father. Thus, everyone has a pair of these tandem-repeat regions. And there may be a different number of repeats on one chromosome compared with the other. Analyzing a person's DNA for several different DNA locations that have tandem repeats can reveal the high degree of individuality that it represents.

MITOCHONDRIA AND MITOCHONDRIAL DNA

The DNA discussed so far is found in the nucleus of the cell, in the chromosomes. In addition to this nuclear DNA, cells also contain DNA in small structures outside the nucleus called "mitochondria." The accompanying diagram of a generalized animal cell shows the nucleus and mitochondria, as well as the other cell structures. Mitochondria contain the cell's energy-processing machinery, but they also contain a small amount of DNA. Mitochondrial DNA (mtDNA) is inherited entirely from one's mother. There is no paternal contribution.

Mitochondrial DNA, unlike its nuclear counterpart, is circular. In that respect it is similar to some bacterial genomes, which consist of a single circular DNA molecule. It is now known that over long periods of time mtDNA occasionally undergoes mutations and that these mutations are stable and passed along from mother to offspring. Anthropologists, scientists who study the variation and evolution of human beings, use mtDNA to follow patterns of human migration over time. Some of the mtDNA codes for specific proteins, but mtDNA also has a region (called the "control region," or "D-loop") that, like some sections of nuclear DNA, is subject to a great deal of polymorphism. It can be divided into two hypervariable regions, designated HV1 and HV2, which are 342 and 268 base pairs (bp) in length, respectively. *Hypervariable* means that these regions are especially prone to random mutations over time, and most of the variability in mtDNA from person to person is found here.

Forensic mtDNA typing is sometimes used in cases when nuclear DNA typing fails or cannot be done. It is also used in trying to identify human remains. Mitochondrial DNA is quite robust in some tissues, especially older or weathered specimens such as old bones. That is the basis for its use in the identification of skeletal remains, which include no soft tissues (and hence no nuclear DNA). In addition, hair shafts contain mtDNA but no nuclear DNA. (Hair roots have nuclear DNA, but many hairs found as evidence have no roots. They are shed from the human body.) So, any DNA analysis on hair shafts must be mtDNA typing.

Mitochondrial DNA Inheritance

Because mitochondria have their own DNA, separate from nuclear DNA, one can speak of a "mitochondrial genome," all the DNA contained in a mitochondrion. Cells have many mitochondria, so there are multiple copies of mtDNA in every cell. The MtDNA genome is significantly smaller than the nuclear genome. The nucleus has about 3.5 billion base pairs in its DNA; the mitochondrion has about 16,500 base pairs in its DNA.

All the variability between people that is forensically useful can essentially be seen by looking through a couple of short sequences in the hypervariable regions. In practice, forensic scientists copy the sequences of interest using the polymerase chain reaction and then analyze the copies. Unlike nuclear DNA typing, which consists of determining the sizes of tandem-repeat regions, mtDNA analysis is sequencing. The variability from person to person in mtDNA consists of a few variations in the base sequence. Thus, the PCR products (the copies) from the hypervariable regions have to be sequenced (the order of the bases in the DNA strand has to be determined). Mitochondrial DNA applications will be discussed further in chapter 5.

POPULATION GENETICS

Mendel's laws of inheritance, discussed earlier, apply to situations involving single matings; that is, the inheritance of one or a few traits or characteristics is studied in the offspring from a single male-female mating. Sometimes, the inheritance of a trait may be followed through several generations, and this progression can be diagrammed in what is called a "pedigree."

But there is another way to look at inheritance. Instead of studying the inheritance of traits in individuals or single matings, one can look at the behavior of a trait or characteristic, or several characteristics, in a large population of individuals. This subject was introduced in chapter 2 (in the sidebar "Using Isoenzyme Types to Include and Exclude Bloodstain Sources") in the context of the frequency of particular blood groups or isoenzyme types. The objective was to figure out how common or rare the blood type and isoenzyme profile was in a population.

Population genetics, like Mendelian genetics, is governed by a set of principles. One of them is that a population rapidly achieves a state known as Hardy-Weinberg equilibrium, in which the frequency of a gene for some characteristic will stabilize and remain constant in a population over many generations. The British mathematician Godfrey Harold Hardy (1877–1947) and the German physician Wilhelm Weinberg (1862–1937) were the scientists who first worked out this principle, in 1907.

This equilibrium is not absolute; it is subject to some conditions. At a practical level the main conditions are a relatively large population, a low rate of mutation, little migration of individuals in or out of the population, and no genes that are either lethal or expressed in dramatically different ways in males and females. (Actually, these conditions are extremely common; they apply to a large number of the genes in many populations.) Why is Hardy-Weinberg equilibrium important for forensic biology? Because it means that the fraction of the population who have the gene for, say, blood type A in the Caucasian population of Chicago will be stable. The proportion is stable and will not change unless something disturbs the equilibrium. If one of the conditions noted above fails to be met, the equilibrium may be disturbed.

Another principle that is important for the way population genetics is used in forensic science is that the probability of independent events is the product of their individual probabilities. (This principle has many other applications as well.) For instance, if the chance of throwing a three with one die is one in six because the die has six faces, then the probability of throwing two three's in a row is one in 36 ($\frac{1}{6} \times \frac{1}{6}$). The reason the numbers can be multiplied is that the events are independent: Nothing about the first throw or its outcome influences what will happen on the second throw. Similarly, in population genetics, if it is known (from experimental testing) that blood type inheritance is independent of PGM isoenzyme inheritance, for example, then one can multiply the frequencies of the types found in a specimen to figure out about how common the combination is expected to be.

The very same principles apply to DNA types. For reasons that will be discussed in chapter 5 current forensic DNA typing involves 13 separate areas (loci) in DNA. They have all been tested to show that they are inherited independent of one another. Geneticists sometimes refer to this independent inheritance across loci as "linkage equilibrium." In addition, population studies have been carried out to determine the frequency of each type at each of the loci. With information like this one can estimate how common a whole DNA profile might be in a population.

It should be noted that there are racial and/or ethnic differences among the frequencies of the types at the different loci used in DNA typing. For example, the frequency of the gene for 18 repeats at a locus called D3S1358 is about 5 percent in African Americans and about 16 percent in

Caucasians. Forensic scientists consider these differences when they calculate how common or rare a profile is expected to be in a population.

METHODS USED TO MANIPULATE AND ANALYZE DNA

Forensic DNA typing was made possible not only by advances in knowledge about DNA structure and function but also by advances in the methods and techniques allowing DNA to be manipulated. Different manipulation methods apply to different DNA-typing technologies. For example, nuclear DNA was first typed using the restriction fragment length polymorphism (RFLP) technique. This procedure did not rely on the polymerase chain reaction but on restriction enzymes and Southern blots. (Southern blotting is discussed later in this chapter.) By contrast, the current typing procedure does rely on PCR but does not make use of restriction enzymes.

Restriction Enzymes

Restriction enzymes were important in the RFLP forensic DNA-typing procedure. Many different bacteria make special enzymes called restriction endonucleases, or restriction enzymes. There are many different restriction enzymes, but they all do one thing: They cut the double-stranded DNA molecule at a specific place. Strictly speaking, the enzyme itself does not "cut" DNA; it catalyzes the hydrolysis of DNA. *Hydrolysis* means that a molecule is separated into two parts and a molecule of water (H_2O) is added in the process. But, as a kind of shorthand, molecular biologists often talk about restriction enzymes "cutting" DNA.

A restriction enzyme cuts DNA at a specific place along the chain because it recognizes a short base sequence of four to seven bases. The restriction enzyme HaeIII, for example, recognizes the sequence ... GGCC ... and EcoR1 recognizes the sequence ... GAATTC. Four additional examples of restriction endonucleases are illustrated in the figure. The heavy arrows in the figure show the cut points in double-stranded DNA at the recognition sequence. The earliest forensic DNA-typing method involved the use of restriction enzymes.

Polymerase Chain Reaction

The polymerase chain reaction, mentioned in chapter 2, is arguably the most important methodological development in the history of molecu-

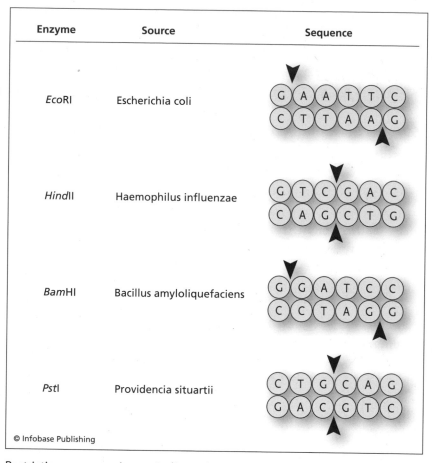

Enzyme	Source	Sequence
*Eco*RI	Escherichia coli	
*Hind*II	Haemophilus influenzae	
*Bam*HI	Bacillus amyloliquefaciens	
*Pst*I	Providencia situartii	

© Infobase Publishing

Restriction enzymes. Arrows indicate the sites at which the enzyme "cuts" the DNA.

lar biology, as evidenced by Kary Mullis's receiving the 1993 Nobel Prize in chemistry for its discovery. PCR imitates and enhances the natural DNA replication process, enabling many copies of a DNA segment to be produced.

The figure shows DNA replication. When DNA replicates naturally, the double strands open up and permit a polymerase enzyme to come in and catalyze copying of the chains. The polymerase cannot copy a DNA strand "from scratch." To work it needs at least a short portion that is double stranded. The short segment that makes a bit of the DNA double stranded is called a primer. Cells make and use natural primers in normal DNA replication.

As explained earlier, double-stranded DNA always obeys the base-pairing rules: T pairs with A, and G pairs with C. PCR simulates the natural process by using a synthesized primer. In this way the scientist controls the DNA segment that will be copied. Suppose the scientist knew that one end of a segment of DNA that he or she wanted to copy had the sequence ATTGGCC. To copy the segment with this end the scientist would synthesize a primer consisting of the complementary strand. This primer (in this case, TAACCGG), a short single-stranded DNA that will

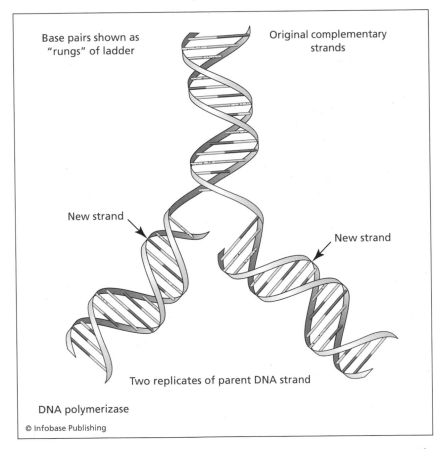

Base pairs shown as "rungs" of ladder

Original complementary strands

New strand

New strand

Two replicates of parent DNA strand

DNA polymerizase

© Infobase Publishing

DNA replication. The original paired strand is copied when new bases pair with their complement, and paired strands form.

locate and base pair with the known sequence, will produce a short segment that is double stranded. This enables a DNA polymerase to copy the rest of the desired strand sequence quickly and accurately.

In other words, the polymerase will finish making the selected DNA segment a double-stranded molecule. In these respects PCR mimics natural DNA replication. The genius of PCR is amplification—that is, making possible many iterations of the process and thus producing millions of copies of a desired sequence. In practice a second primer would have to be synthesized, and it would be complementary to the other end of the DNA segment one wanted to copy. In addition, the second primer would prime (be complementary) to the other strand of double-stranded DNA. In the figure the primers look very short, but actual primers are usually about 18 to 24 bases long.

PCR is possible because of a special type of DNA polymerase called a "thermostable polymerase." Most enzymes are quickly inactivated if heated, but these special polymerases are not. The original thermostable DNA polymerase was called "Taq," a shortened version of the name of the bacterium that it came from.

There are three steps in one PCR cycle: denaturation, primer annealing, and chain extension. When DNA is heated to 203°F (95°C) (almost the boiling temperature of water), the strands will separate. This is called "denaturation," or melting. If the solution is simply cooled, the strands will come back together, but if primers are added to the solution as it cools down to around 122–140°F (50–60°C), the outcome will be different. The original strands will not go back together; instead, the primers will adhere to the single strands at the location where the sequences are exactly complementary to them, a process called "primer annealing." Then, by raising the temperature to about 161.6°F (72°C) and including a thermostable DNA polymerase in the solution (along with other required chemicals), one can induce copying of the strand of DNA flanked by the primers. This process is called "chain extension." If the temperature is once again increased to 203°F (95°C), the DNA will again denature, and the whole process can be repeated.

Each such repetition is called a PCR cycle. All three steps in a PCR cycle—denaturation, primer annealing, and chain extension (copying)—are controlled by temperature. An instrument called a thermal cycler is used for PCR. All it really does is quickly raise and lower the temperatures in the reaction tubes.

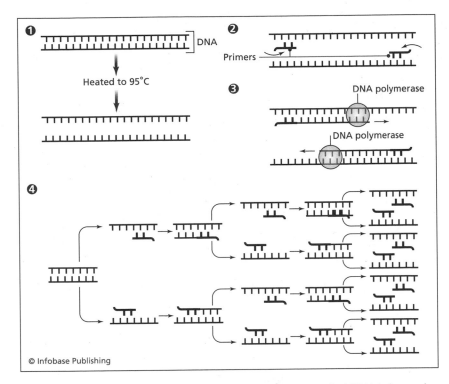

Polymerase Chain Reaction (PCR). 1. When double-stranded DNA is heated to 95°C (203°F), the strands separate. 2. Two chemically synthesized primers, with base sequences complementary to the sequences flanking the DNA region to be copied, can attach to the separated strands by base pairing when the temperature is lowered to about 60°C. 3. As the temperature is raised to about 72°C, the DNA polymerase enzyme catalyzes the synthesis of new strands of DNA downstream of each primer. 4. Repeating this heating, cooling, heating, cycle over and over doubles the number of DNA molecules synthesized in each cycle. After 30 cycles, there will be more than a billion copies of double-stranded DNA molecules defined at their ends by the primers.

The cycling is repeated until millions of copies of the desired DNA segment have been synthesized. The number of DNA segments doubles in each cycle, so the number of copies grows geometrically (by powers of two). That is, it increases from two to four to eight to 16, and so on. After 30 cycles of PCR there are more than 1 billion copies of the DNA segment. This is one reason PCR is so useful in forensic work: Very small amounts of starting material (the evidence) can be amplified into many identical copies, making successful analysis possible. Most forensic PCR-typing techniques are optimized for about one nanogram (one-billionth of a gram) of DNA. One nanogram is approximately the quantity of DNA present in 100 cells.

Gel Methods

Scientists often need to see whether DNA was successfully prepared from cells or tissues in evidence, how big the molecules are, and how much DNA is in the preparation. Gel methods are commonly used for these purposes. Gel methods provide a way of visualizing DNA.

DNA is a very large molecule that is highly negatively charged. As a result it can be moved by electrophoresis in a gel medium. Electrophoresis is a procedure that uses an electronic field to move big, charged molecules. Agarose gels (similar in consistency to Jell-O) provide a good medium for DNA movement in an electric field. An electrophoresis setup consists of the agarose gel placed in a chamber that separates a positive from a negative compartment and is filled with a solution containing charged particles. The diagram on page 33 shows an electrophoresis setup. A power supply sets up a current in the gel. DNA specimens placed in wells near the negative end will migrate toward the positive end, because DNA is very negatively charged and because unlike charges attract.

Different sized DNA molecules travel different speeds and distances. The larger the DNA molecule, the more slowly it migrates. Thus, the distance a DNA molecule travels gives an indication of how big it is. To help in these estimates scientists typically add standards and calibrators (proteins of known size) to the gel and run them along with the specimens. One factor affecting the size of DNA fragments is degradation. Environmental exposure can cause the DNA in a forensic specimen to degrade, to break into smaller fragments. As a result the specimen will contain an array of different sized DNA molecules. Whereas intact, undegraded DNA appears as a tight band on the agarose gel, degraded DNA is visible as a streak.

DNA is not, however, visible by itself, in a test tube, or on a gel. One must add another material to the DNA to make it visible, and certain dyes that can tuck themselves into the folds of the double helix are used for this purpose. When the DNA-dye complex is illuminated by ultraviolet (UV) light, the DNA fluoresces, so it can be seen. The gels themselves change and degrade over time, so they cannot be kept and stored. Consequently, lab scientists regularly take pictures of these UV-illuminated gels to make a permanent record of the outcome of electrophoresis. Furthermore, photography can actually improve visibility of the results. The fluorescent DNA appears white on an otherwise black background in the photo, and it is sometimes easier to see things in the picture than on the gel itself.

Southern Blots

As DNA analysis methods were being developed, it was common to separate DNA fragments of different sizes on agarose gels, as described in the preceding section. Many times, though, scientists wanted to do further testing steps that just would not work in gels. A biochemist named Edwin Southern came up with a method to solve this problem in 1975.

Southern's method employs a membrane made of nitrocellulose or nylon, which is laid onto the gel after the DNA fragments have been separated. The gel and membrane are then placed into a buffer solution (a solution that resists change in pH), and some absorbent material is placed on top of the membrane. The absorbent material draws the solution upward, through the gel and through the membrane, but the DNA fragments in the gel are too big to go through the membrane, so they stick to it. Because the membrane is the same size as the gel, it retains the original position and orientation of the DNA fragments in the gel.

Once the DNA fragments are on the membrane, they are stable and cannot easily be removed. Furthermore, the membrane is tough and resilient, allowing scientists to do further tests on the DNA right on the membrane. This process of transferring DNA fragments from a gel to a membrane is called "Southern blotting," and the resulting membrane is often just called a "blot." This procedure was an important part of the earliest kind of forensic DNA typing, and it is still used regularly in research labs.

Separation, Labeling, and Detection of DNA Segments

Suppose a scientist were looking for a certain sequence pattern in a mixture of DNA fragments of different sizes. The mixture could be separated by electrophoresis on an agarose gel and then fixed on a membrane by Southern blotting. Then, in order to locate the desired DNA sequence pattern on the blot, a single-stranded segment of DNA called a "probe" could be added directly to the blot.

A probe is a single strand of DNA with a sequence complementary to the target strand of DNA. There are methods to easily label the probe—and thus visualize the target sequence that the probe binds with—using radioactive phosphorus-32 (^{32}P) labels. Once the probe is labeled, it can be placed in a solution with the membrane-containing mixture of all the separated DNA fragments. Under controlled conditions the probe will base pair only with the exactly complementary sequence; this process is called "hybridization." The reason that the probe can base pair (hybridize) with its complementary sequence directly on the membrane is that the Southern blotting process has already denatured the DNA on the membrane, that is, rendered it single stranded.

The excess probe and solution can then be washed away, leaving the membrane with a radioactive probe adhering to one DNA fragment. The scientist can now visualize the target DNA sequence by placing this membrane against a sheet of X-ray film. The radioactivity exposes the film just as X-rays would. When the film is developed, it shows an image of the DNA fragment that had the radioactive label on it. This process, illustrated in the diagram, is called "autoradiography." The first forensic DNA typing was done in this way. But radioactive materials such as ^{32}P pose a health hazard, so it is expensive and cumbersome to handle and store them in the safe, legal way. Later, a method using light-emitting (chemiluminescent) probes was developed so scientists could avoid having to work with the radioactive phosphorus.

As already discussed, scientists can separate DNA fragments of different sizes using electrophoresis on agarose gels, but the electrophoresis can also be carried out in tiny capillaries that are filled with a solution of buffer and polymers (somewhat comparable to agarose). This process is capillary electrophoresis (CE) and has some significant advantages over traditional gel electrophoresis. One is that heat does not build up as much in the capillary. Heat buildup is a problem in electrophoresis, both because it can denature protein or DNA molecules and because it can change the properties of the medium (the agarose or buffer solution) in a way that affects the migration proper-

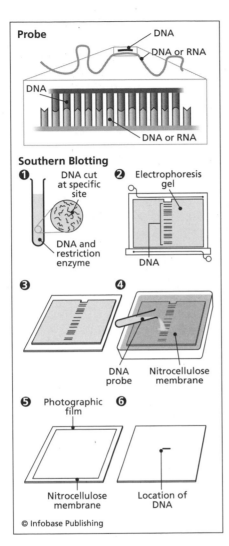

Probe

DNA

DNA or RNA

DNA

DNA or RNA

Southern Blotting

❶ DNA cut at specific site

DNA and restriction enzyme

❷ Electrophoresis gel

DNA

❸

❹

DNA probe

Nitrocellulose membrane

❺ Photographic film

❻

Nitrocellulose membrane

Location of DNA

© Infobase Publishing

DNA probes and Southern blotting. Probe: Short sequences of single-stranded DNA, 20-50 nucleotides (building blocks) long, can be chemically synthesized and them made radioactive or fluorescent. This DNA can base pair with a complementary DNA or RNA strand, labeling it as either radioactive or luminescent. Southern blotting: 1. The DNA is fragmented by the addition of a restriction enzyme (biological catalyst that cuts DNA at specific sites). 2. The fragments are next separated, according to their length, into invisible bands on electrophoresis gel. 3. The separated DNA fragments can then be transferred to a nitrocellulose or nylon membrane. The DNA molecules are made to stick permanently to the membrane. 4. When a radioactive DNA probe solution is added to the membrane and then gently washed off, some of the probes will remain attached to any DNA fragments that have a complementary sequence. 5. The membrane is placed against a photographic film. 6. The film darkens wherever the radioactive DNA probe has bound to the membrane. The probe has identified which DNA fragment contains the complementary DNA sequence for the probe.

ties of the molecules. If heat buildup is not controlled, it can affect the reproducibility of electrophoresis.

Another advantage of CE is that it permits certain types of analysis involving detection of fluorescent labels to be done in the same instrument. This is possible because the fragments emerge one by one from the narrow capillary tube. Capillary electrophoresis (described further in chapter 5) is now widely used in forensic DNA typing.

CONCLUDING REMARKS

The story of DNA structure and function provides the molecular basis for our understanding of genetics. Genetics and inheritance work through DNA. DNA structure is the reason for human individuality. DNA analysis is important to forensic science because its analysis can essentially individualize biological evidence. And, it is through genetics and population genetics that the ability of DNA analysis to tie an item of biological evidence to a particular person can be understood.

4

Blood and Body Fluids: Preliminary Testing

This chapter discusses the issues of evidence handling and of the identification and species testing of blood or physiological fluid evidence that precede DNA typing. Blood patterns are discussed here. Blood patterns can be analyzed at scenes, or in the laboratory, or both. Blood pattern analysis is a scene reconstruction activity. It can help establish how bloodstains were formed and provide indications of force and direction of blood spatter.

PRINCIPLES OF HANDLING EVIDENCE

As noted in chapter 1, many of the activities in a public forensic science lab can be grouped under the heading of criminalistics. One of these is evidence handling. Some general principles apply to handling and evaluating any kind of evidence. These principles relate to documentation, chain of custody, packaging, preservation, preventing contamination, and safety issues.

Documentation means that there are good records of what an evidence item is and exactly where it came from, as well as sufficient labeling so that it can be tracked from place to place. Items collected at a crime scene may be stored in a police department evidence storage facility, then removed and taken to a laboratory. At the laboratory the items are kept in secure storage facilities except when they are taken out to be analyzed. Following analysis they may be returned to police evidence storage. If the case to which the items relate goes to trial, the evidence is removed from police evidence storage and transferred to court evidence storage. From there it may be removed and taken to the courtroom during the trial, then placed back in storage. Documentation provides ways to track the items through these transfers. There must be sufficient documentation to establish that an item brought into the courtroom as an exhibit is the same item that police seized at the crime scene or other original location. This process of ensuring that it is the same item is sometimes called the "chain of custody." It amounts to documentation that shows where the item was at all times since its original seizure.

Packaging has two important goals. One is simply to hold the item in a container that will preserve it for subsequent analysis. The other is to prevent undetected tampering with or any contamination of the evidence. The second goal is achieved by proper sealing. Anyone who opens the packaging (such as the forensic scientist who analyzes it) writes his or her initials and the date on the package and then reseals the evidence.

Contamination means that something is inadvertently introduced into the evidence. It is possible for biological evidence to be contaminated by the external environment or by actions or events that occur before any crime scene investigation. Crime scene investigators have no control over that kind of contamination. What crime scene investigators must take steps to avoid is contamination during the investigation or evidence collection. Contamination is a potential problem with certain kinds of evidence. Ideally, evidence reaches the laboratory in its original condition. Crime scene personnel take precautions accordingly. They wear gloves and sometimes other protective clothing to avoid contaminating any evidence. The other side of this coin is the safety of the people who handle the evidence. Evidence can be hazardous. It could be caustic, toxic, or potentially explosive. It can also contain potentially infectious bacteria or viruses. So, evidence handling techniques are designed to protect both the evidence from the handler and the handler from the evidence.

All these considerations apply to handling biological evidence, such as blood or other body fluids. The biggest danger is spoilage because bacteria or fungi infect and destroy the evidence. To prevent that spoilage biological evidence must be thoroughly dry before packaging, and it needs to be packaged in paper containers. Paper containers are not airtight. Some plastic containers (such as Ziploc bags) are. Biological evidence can be stored in refrigerators as well. But even if it is stored at room temperature, it is generally stable provided it was thoroughly dried and packaged in paper containers. In some laboratories biological evidence is kept frozen to preserve it. Because of space and resource considerations, it may be possible to freeze only a small, representative specimen of the evidence.

PRELIMINARY EXAMINATIONS: SEARCHING, IDENTIFICATION, AND SPECIES TESTING

The following are three steps in the preliminary evaluation and examination of biological evidence:

1. searching and evaluation of evidence and selection of specimens

2. identification

3. species testing

The steps are termed *preliminary* because they are necessary but done before any DNA analysis. A forensic scientist must know what a stain is, and whether it is human, before proceeding to DNA typing. Sometimes these preliminary evaluation and testing activities are called "forensic biology" to distinguish them from DNA typing. Thus, the term *forensic biology* can have the broader meaning being used in this book, or it can have the narrower meaning just noted.

Searching and Evaluation of Evidence and Selection of Specimens

A variety of different items are submitted to the forensic biology section of the laboratory. An article of clothing is typical, but it could also be a sheet, a pillowcase, a car seat, or another item that investigators think may have evidence on it. These items have to be searched in the laboratory. Sometimes it is fairly easy to see biological traces on an object or item, and other times it is not. Analysts may use ultraviolet or laser or other intense light sources to illuminate evidence items. Biological stains may fluoresce and thus be more visible under these alternative light sources. At this stage analysts may use preliminary tests, such as the phenolphthalin test for blood or the acid phosphatase for seminal fluid, on the evidence to guide them in finding the biological traces and stains. These tests and how they work are described later in this chapter.

Besides finding the biological stains on evidence items, analysts must sometimes make choices about what to take for further analysis. Suppose a pair of pants is submitted with 200 small blood spots on one of the legs. It is not realistic to think the laboratory has the resources to isolate and analyze every one of them. The analyst has to select a sample of the stains to analyze further. Knowledge of bloodstain patterns can help here. The patterns formed by blood droplets in their flight through the air follow established principles. Knowing how blood patterns form can help an analyst figure out that a group of stains was likely formed by the same blood source. Blood patterns are discussed later in the chapter.

This initial selection of specimens from the evidence for further analysis is extremely important. During this process the analyst is relating the evidence to the case and to the question that the analysis is trying to help answer. Mistakes or bad judgments at this stage can mean that nothing informative will come from the analysis.

Another concept related to the selection of specimens for analysis is called "best evidence." It is a given that the laboratory does not have the resources to analyze every stain on every submitted item. The best evidence concept is usually applied to sexual assault evidence. Suppose a sexual assault case is submitted, and there is a bed sheet with biological stains, underwear with biological stains, and a vaginal swab taken from the complainant by a forensic nurse. If the vaginal swab tests positive for semen, the best evidence concept suggests that it may be the only item sent forward for DNA typing. The reason is that the laboratory's task is to help establish that a sexual assault actually happened and then to try to identify the assailant. This task can be completed unequivocally by successful DNA typing of the vaginal swab. If the swab analysis is successful, it is unnecessary to subject the other items to DNA analysis, as additional analysis will not shed any more light on the question the laboratory is tasked to answer.

Identification

The second step in the preliminary examination is identification. The word *identification* sometimes means "individualization." People might say, for example, that "a body was identified," meaning that the human remains are those of a particular person. Here, however, the word is being used to mean "classification." Two types of tests are used for this purpose: preliminary tests and confirmatory tests. The difference is that preliminary tests are usually quick, sensitive, and convenient but not definitive. For example, a positive preliminary test for blood shows that the specimen could be blood; however, materials that are not blood can also give a positive test result. In other words, false positives are possible. Positive confirmatory tests, on the other hand, prove what is the blood or body fluid specimen.

The most common specimens coming into the forensic biology laboratory are, or might be, blood, semen, vaginal swabs, saliva, or urine. There are preliminary and confirmatory tests for blood, and there are preliminary tests for the other body fluids. As of 2007 the only nonblood body fluid for which there was a confirmatory test was semen. This means that the forensic lab cannot prove that a stain is saliva, urine, or vaginal secretion. It can report only that a stain gave a positive preliminary test and therefore could be the body fluid for which the test was designed.

The most characteristic feature of blood is hemoglobin, and forensic tests for blood are based on detecting hemoglobin or its components. Hemoglobin is the protein that transports oxygen between the lungs and all the tissues and cells of the body. Hemoglobin consists of two parts, "heme" (which carries the oxygen) and "globin" (the protein portion). The preliminary forensic blood identification tests are really tests for heme. They use certain dye substances that, when mixed with peroxide, will change color in a chemical reaction called "oxidation." There are protein enzymes in nature that will speed up this reaction, but heme will also speed up the reaction. Remember that enzymes are catalysts; they speed up reactions that are otherwise slow. Likewise, heme is acting like a catalyst in this reaction, so forensic scientists call these tests "catalytic." They have been used for well over 100 years. A number of different dye substances work, several of which are commonly used in forensic science laboratories. They are orthotolidine, phenolphthalin, leucomalachite green, and tetramethylbenzidine. Made up in the proper solutions, these chemicals change color in a positive test.

The tests are often done on the tip of a cotton swab. A clean Q-tip can be moistened with distilled water, then used to swab up just a bit of a suspected bloodstain. Transferring a small bit of the suspected stain to the Q-tip for testing avoids contaminating the evidence with any testing reagents. The other end of the Q-tip serves as a blank control. It has nothing on it except the cotton, and no color change is expected. This blank end is serving as a control because its failure to give the color change shows that the cotton itself is not causing the reaction. These catalytic tests are quick and convenient, and analysts use them while searching evidence items. They can be used at scenes as well. Another testing chemical sometimes used in preliminary testing is luminol. Luminol in solution under certain conditions will luminesce, or produce a blue light. Chemists call this chemiluminescence. One of the things that will make it luminesce is hemoglobin. As a result luminol can be used for preliminary blood testing. It is especially useful at crime scenes, where blood traces are present only in tiny quantities not visible to the naked eye. For instance, if someone has "cleaned up" blood from a surface, there is enough still there to make the luminol glow. Not only that, but the luminescence will show the bloodstain pattern.

Identification testing must also be done for physiological fluid stains. The most common body fluid submitted to the laboratory is semen. The semen is always submitted on a vaginal swab or slide, on clothing, or some other object as a stain. These items must be tested for the presence of semen. There is a preliminary test, the acid phosphatase test, that an analyst can use to see whether semen might be present. Acid phosphatase is an enzyme usually present in large quantities in the seminal fluid. A test involving a simple color change is available for acid phosphatase, and forensic biologists often use it to screen items of evidence—to see whether semen might be present. Finding acid phosphatase does not prove that semen is present, but it prompts further testing. The reason the acid phosphatase test is presumptive is that the enzyme occurs in things other than semen. The test detects the acid phosphatase enzyme, not semen specifically. If acid phosphatase from some other source is present, the test will register positive, and such a result would be a false positive.

When a woman reports that she has been sexually assaulted, she is ordinarily taken to a clinic for an examination, which includes collecting vaginal specimens. Her clothing, samples of hair, and other specimens may also be collected. A sexual assault evidence collection kit, as described in the sidebar, is typically used for this purpose. The kit is designed to make the collection of evidence from a complainant's person easy for the nurse or doctor. In the process it allows all the specimens to be properly separated and packaged, following the standard evidence handling guidelines discussed earlier.

The forensic science laboratory receives the completed sexual assault evidence kit and does the analysis of the specimens. In a sexual assault case the analyst first tests for semen on the vaginal specimens, usually collected on swabs similar to Q-tips. The swab has the woman's fluids and cells on it, and if there was any semen, it should have some of that as well. Material from the swab is used to make a slide. The slide might be made either in the clinic or in the forensic laboratory. It is a regular glass microscope slide onto which material from the swab is applied. If semen can be identified on the slide or the swab, it means that semen was present in the woman's vagina at the time she was examined. This finding is consistent with sexual intercourse within about 72 to 96 hours prior to the examination. The forensic analyst may examine the woman's underwear, too, which can contain drainage stains that have semen. If the swab is positive for the presence of semen, it is normally unnecessary to examine the underwear. The materials submitted for analysis may also include swabbings of stains taken from external areas of the body that need to be examined for semen. Oral and anal swabs and slides, and fingernail cuttings or scrapings, are examined if submitted. Hairs and debris or trace evidence from outer clothing are generally examined in a different section of the laboratory.

The critical questions for the laboratory in a sexual assault case are, first, whether semen is present, and second, whether its source can be identified. Identifying semen on the vaginal specimen is sufficient to establish the elements of the crime. Other items need not be examined. Doing so will add nothing to the laboratory's findings. Should the vagi-

Sexual Assault Evidence Collection Kits

The purpose of sexual assault evidence collection kits is to make the task of collecting evidence from a complainant, or from a suspect, easier for the clinicians. A lot of discussion and planning usually go into the design of one of these kits. Typically, they are specific to a particular state or, occasionally, to a large city. Many states have passed laws creating coordinating committees for the investigation of and response to sexual assault. Among the responsibilities of these committees is the specification of evidence kit design. The committees usually have representatives from the forensic science laboratory, the clinical personnel who attend to complainants, the prosecutor's office, and victim services agencies.

The so-called kit is really just a large box or other container that has many smaller containers within it. Each container has a specific purpose: It is designed to package a specific item of evidence. The kits are designed to be used according to the standard principles of evidence handling and packaging. All the biological evidence containers are non-airtight paper. Labeling information is preprinted on the packaging. Instructions for the clinician are included in the kit. In some places training videotapes have been made to help clinicians prepare for their duties in these circumstances. Some jurisdictions have adopted the practice of having forensic nurses conduct the clinical examination of sexual assault complainants. Forensic nurses called sexual assault nurse examiners (SANEs) are specially trained to carry out these duties. In jurisdictions that have adopted the practice of using SANEs, the clinics for sexual assault complainants are often separate from regular emergency departments in hospitals.

Evidence is always collected from a complainant of sexual assault if the assault happened within a certain amount of time of its being reported. This amount of time varies by jurisdiction but is usually about 72 hours (three days). The notion is that after three days, there will not be any evidence left in or on the victim's body. Evidence may also be collected from a suspect if he is apprehended soon enough after the incident. Sexual assault victims are usually women but not always. Men can be assaulted by other men. Some states have designed evidence collection kits that can be used for men or women, while others have separate kits for the two sexes.

The kit usually makes provision for collection of all the evidence that is associated with the body, as well as clothing and certain standards (knowns) that will be needed by the lab for its testing. The following table lists items typically found in a "victim" kit and a brief description of the purpose for collecting them.

Item	Purpose of Collection
Debris or trace items on outer clothing	May associate victim with scene, corroborating victim's statements
Outer clothing	May have biological stains
Underclothing	May have biological stains (as from drainage)
Vaginal swab	Recovery of semen for testing
Vaginal smear (made from swab)	Used to look for sperm cells microscopically
Oral swab	Recovery of semen for testing (if oral sex is reported)
Oral smear (made from swab)	Used to look for sperm cells microscopically
Rectal swab	Recovery of semen for testing (if anal sex is reported)
Rectal smear (made from swab)	Used to look for sperm cells microscopically
Head hair specimen	Known standard—may have transferred to perpetrator or his clothing or belongings
Pubic hair specimen	Known standard—may have transferred to perpetrator or his underclothing
Fingernail cuttings or scrapings	May contain blood or tissue from perpetrator
Swabs of stains on the body	May have been deposited on the body by perpetrator

(continues)

(continued)

Item	Purpose of Collection
Blood specimen or buccal (inner cheek) swab	Known standard to obtain victim's DNA profile

The same kit can be used for a male victim or for a suspect. In the case of a suspect the swabs can be used for the penis. If the suspect has been apprehended quickly, there may be DNA from the victim still on his penis, assuming he had vaginal intercourse with her.

Not every item in the kit may be collected. If the complainant says that there was no oral or anal contact, for example, those specimens will usually not be collected.

There are consent forms that must be completed by complainants in most jurisdictions, and they may be included in the kits. A complainant must consent to being examined and treated, and, in addition, must often separately consent to having the kit specimens sent to the forensic lab.

Sometimes victims believe they have been drugged. If so, a urine specimen may also be collected and sent for drug testing. A separate consent for this may be required, depending on the jurisdiction. The reason for the separate consent for drug testing is to inform the victim that the lab tests for all drugs, not just so-called date-rape drugs. Some complainants do not want the lab to find out they have been using drugs recreationally and may not consent to this testing.

Besides evidence collection, clinicians attending to sexual assault complainants also take a medical history and treat any injuries that the person may have sustained. The medical history can help guide the evidence-collection procedures. For example, if the complainant states that she was not orally assaulted, oral specimens need not be taken.

Finally, clinicians also attend to other potential medical issues. Tests for pregnancy and for sexually transmitted diseases are frequently part of the protocols. Sexual assault evidence collection kits are intended to facilitate thorough documentation and follow-up of assault complaints.

nal specimen be negative for semen, the other evidence must be examined thoroughly.

Semen is a complex body fluid. It is the male's reproductive fluid. It has a liquid part called seminal fluid and a cellular part, the spermatozoa, or male reproductive cells. Men may have 20 million to as much as 250 million sperm cells per milliliter of semen. (A milliliter is a unit of volume, on the order of 20 drops from an eyedropper.) The average range is probably 40 million to 60 million per milliliter, but there is considerable variation from person to person as well as variation within an individual over time. Some men have diseases that cause them to produce much less sperm or no sperm. Others have surgery (vasectomy) to sever the ducts that normally carry sperm cells. After the operation they are sterile; they have no sperm in their semen.

The forensic biologist uses a microscope to examine the slide evidence described earlier for sperm. Sperm cells are quite small, and the microscope has to be capable of magnifications of the order of 400X to 500X to make them visible. The photograph shows spermatozoa as seen under a microscope. The photograph is shown black and white, but in the lab the sperm are colored using dyes because dyeing makes them easier to find under the microscope. A stain called "Christmas tree" is popular in forensic labs. It makes the sperm heads red, the midpieces green, and the tails blue.

The presence of sperm cells proves that the evidence specimen contains semen. As noted, however, there can be semen with no sperm cells. Taking that possibility into consideration, the analyst does a different confirmatory test, one that detects a specific protein (p30, or prostatic antigen) in the seminal fluid. Finding this protein also proves that there is semen in the evidence.

Saliva is one's oral fluid, and it bathes the inside of the mouth. It is produced by three pairs of salivary glands. Like other body fluids, it contains a variety of biochemical compounds. An enzyme called amylase is the most abundant protein in saliva, and its presence has long been used as an indication of the presence of saliva. Amylase is an enzyme that catalyzes the breakdown of starch. Starch is a carbohydrate storage compound in plants and a constituent of many foods. There are several tests available for amylase that can be used. Finding amylase does not prove that saliva was present in the specimen, only that it could have

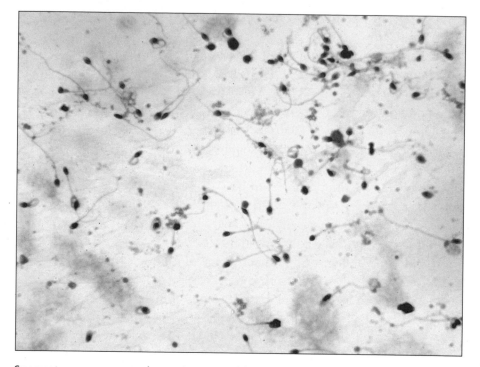

Spermatozoa as seen under a microscope (*Courtesy of the author*)

been. There is no confirmatory test for saliva. If a suspect stain is not semen (that is, if tests for semen are negative), then the stain may be tested to see if it could be saliva. Occasionally, a vaginal swab is tested for amylase (possible saliva) because the victim reports that the perpetrator assaulted her by forcing oral sex.

Another body fluid analysts may test stains for occasionally is urine. Urine is mostly water, but it has a few compounds in it that can indicate its presence. In forensic laboratories analysts usually test for urea or creatinine as indicators that a specimen might contain urine. These compounds are present in urine but are not exclusive to it. There is no confirmatory test for urine.

Some of the specimens coming into the forensic lab do not have to be subjected to identification testing. For example, a filter on a smoked cigarette has some saliva and cells on it. The evidence context—what the evidence item is—tells the analyst what the body fluid is. There would be no reason to test the cigarette butt for blood or any other fluid. Similarly, the vaginal swab collected as part of a sexual assault evidence collection kit does not have to be tested for vaginal epithelial cells. Someone in the clinic actually took the swabbing from a person, so the lab analyst knows what it is and that the cells are present without any testing. The known specimens that have to be collected from people in cases do not need to be identified. For years the known specimens that were taken from known persons were blood specimens. Sometimes they may still be. But for DNA all that is needed are some known cells from the person, and cheek swabbings (buccal swabs) fill this need without having to draw any blood.

The forensic lab findings alone are not sufficient to establish a sexual assault complaint or charge. Finding sperm or semen on the vaginal swab shows only that it is there. It could have gotten there through consensual sexual relations or through a sexual assault. By the same token failure to find sperm or semen on a vaginal swab does not prove that sexual relations or sexual assault did not happen. The man could have used a condom or may have failed to deposit any semen. Generally, investigators and sometimes prosecutors and defense attorneys must sort through the laboratory findings and the statements by the people involved to try to determine what actually happened.

Species Testing

Because bloodstain specimens can sometimes be from animals, species tests are generally done on them before they are analyzed further. Many of the bloodstains submitted to a laboratory are indeed human, but there are circumstances in which animal blood can become evidence. For instance, in hit-and-run cases where blood is found on a vehicle, the motorist may claim to have hit an animal. Game law enforcement cases are another situation where the blood of game animals may be important evidence. People sometimes claim that suspicious bloodstains are of animal blood.

All the species tests used in forensic laboratories for more than a hundred years were based on the principles of immunology. These basic principles—the science of antigens and antibodies—were established in the late 19th and early 20th centuries. The most important implications of those discoveries had to do with immunity against infectious diseases: figuring out ways to vaccinate people. In the process, however, many laboratory methods involving antigens and antibodies proved to be very helpful tests.

The proteins of a particular species, such as humans or horses or cats, are different from the proteins of other species. Each immune system can tell them apart. If the blood proteins from a human or a cat are injected into a living rabbit, the rabbit's immune system will see them as "foreign" and will produce antibodies to them. Scientists can collect those antibodies from the rabbit and use them as tools to test whether bloodstains came from humans or cats. When antigens and their corresponding antibodies combine and bind, several things can happen. One possible result is that they precipitate out and form a visible product.

One version of a forensic blood species test is called an Ouchterlony dish, named after Örjan Ouchterlony (1914–2004), the Swedish scientist who first worked out this procedure. It is usually performed in an agarose gel, into which are punched six wells configured like the corners of a hexagon, which surround a center well. The center well often contains an antibody solution, and the surrounding wells contain solutions of antigen that one wants to test against the center-well antibody. A white precipitation line develops between the center well and any of the surrounding wells that contain the homologous antigen. (Homologous means physically and functionally similar.) In a typical forensic test four peripheral wells would contain extracts from unknown bloodstains, and the center well would contain antihuman antibody. Two of the peripheral wells are used for positive and negative controls; in this example human bloodstain extract serves as a control for a positive result, and any nonhuman bloodstain extract serves as a negative control. If bloodstain extracts from a case were negative against antihuman, and there was any reason to suspect that the stains could be nonhuman, more testing would be required. Separate Ouchterlony dishes could be run with antiserum for other species, such as dog, cat, horse, cow, and so on.

If bloodstains are shown to be nonhuman, the case is probably finished from the laboratory's point of view. Such findings would generally tend to support, or to contradict, the statements someone has made to the police. If bloodstains are tested and found to be human, they are ready for DNA typing.

As the number of cases and evidence items pouring into forensic laboratories has increased, backlogs have developed, and labs have attempted to devise strategies to work on evidence more efficiently without sacrificing rigor. One such strategy is to begin tests on blood with human-specific DNA profiling. Nearly all bloodstained items that come into the lab are human and are thus going to be DNA profiled. Some of the loci used in developing the DNA profile are human specific. (Actually, they are primate specific, but nonhuman primate blood is not normally a big concern.) If a human-specific locus gives a type, the specimen must have been human. By this reasoning a separate time-consuming species test can be avoided. Another test that can establish that a specimen is human is RT-PCR. This technique, which is used to determine the quantity of human DNA, will be discussed in chapter 5.

BLOOD PATTERNS

As already explained, most of the material in this book on blood and physiological fluids has to do with identifying them and using DNA analysis to help figure out who may or may not have deposited them. The terms *identification* and *individualization* describe two of these activities. There is a third activity, reconstruction, that can also be an important part of a forensic case analysis.

Violent events involving bloodshed can produce bloodstain patterns, sometimes also called blood-spatter patterns. Certain blood patterns are a predictable result of certain specific events. This is because when blood is shed, then acted upon by physical forces, it follows established physical laws. Accordingly, examination of blood patterns can provide information about the amount of force that caused the spatter, the angle of flight of blood droplets, and the type of action or event that produced the bloodstain.

Bloodstain patterns can first be classified as low velocity, medium velocity, and high velocity. The photographs show examples of low-, medium-, and high-velocity blood-spatter patterns. These three categories are defined by the amount of force that acts on the blood to produce the pattern. Blood dripping from an injured person falls to the ground or floor. A drop of blood falling through the air behaves like any object falling through the air: Its velocity increases as it falls, but only to a maximum value, called "terminal velocity."

In fact, blood falling to the ground or floor from an injured person does not travel a sufficient distance to reach terminal velocity. It hits

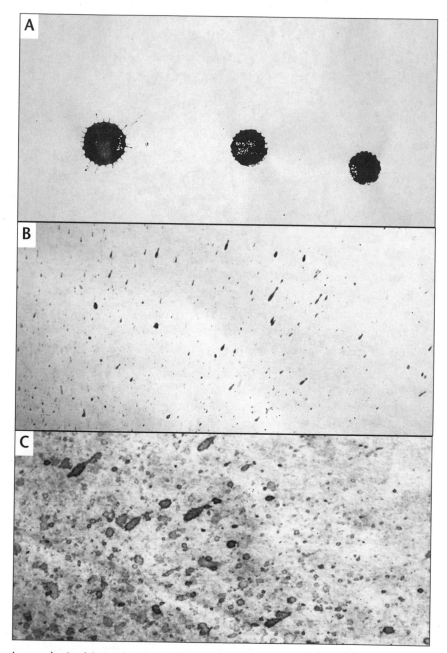

Low-velocity (a), medium-velocity (b), and high-velocity (c) blood-spatter patterns. There is no scale in the pictures, but the blood drops become smaller going from low to medium to high velocity, and there are many more of them within the same area. *(Courtesy of the author)*

the ground or floor first. The only force acting on this blood is gravity. Low-velocity blood patterns are the result of the force of gravity alone and are typically circular. The size of the stain circle is determined by the absorbency of the surface. On a nonabsorbent surface like linoleum or paper, the size of the circle is related to the volume of blood in the droplet that caused the stain. But if a droplet hits an absorbent surface like a piece of cotton cloth, the circle's size has to do with how much it spreads out as this material absorbs it. Droplets that fall from greater heights onto nonabsorbent surfaces can have satellite droplet patterns surrounding the main circle.

Medium-velocity blood patterns result from force being applied to a pool of blood. One example is blunt-force injury to a victim's head. In a blunt force injury a person is hit with a blunt object, like a piece of board, a baseball bat, or a brick. The first blow injures the victim, causing blood to pool at the site of the wound. If the victim is hit again, and the object strikes the blood pool, the blood will be spattered in all directions. The force involved causes the blood to be broken up into smaller droplets. Accordingly, a medium-velocity pattern typically consists of many small droplets of blood. Another example of an action that could cause medium-velocity blood spatter is stomping one's shoe into a pool of blood at a scene.

Lastly, high-velocity blood patterns result from events involving extreme forces. Two common examples are gunshot wounds and explosions. When a person is shot, the projectile that hits the victim is traveling at very high velocity, and it strikes the body with great force. This force causes the blood to be broken up into very small droplets, some as small as the droplets from an aerosol spray can. There are a large number of these small droplets in a high-velocity spatter pattern. Since the velocity category of a blood pattern is determined by the amount of force that produced the spatter, recognizing which category a bloodstain pattern belongs to provides information about how much force was involved in its production.

The angle at which a blood droplet strikes a surface can help determine where it came from. If a blood droplet impacts a surface perpendicularly (at a 90° angle) the resulting stain will be round (circular). If the droplet hits the surface at any other angle, however, the resulting stain will be oval, or egg-shaped (elliptical). The figure shows that stain patterns become increasingly elliptical as the angle of incidence

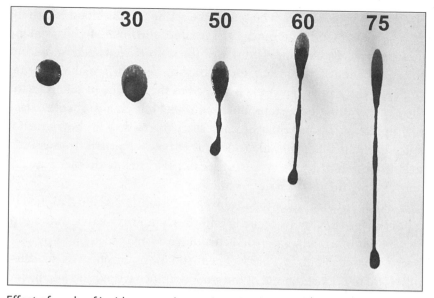

Effect of angle of incidence on the resulting blood-spatter pattern. The numbers represent the angle at which a drop was traveling with respect to the perpendicular (straight down) line when it struck the surface, such as 0°, 30°, or 75°. *(Courtesy of the author)*

increases. At the larger angles there are "trail" patterns below the ellipse shape, resulting from excess blood that has run down the surface at the steeper angles after the droplet hit. Forensic scientists can measure how elliptical the stain pattern is and use these measurements to calculate the angle of impact. To make the calculations work the angle of impact is expressed not with respect to the surface itself, but with respect to an imaginary line perpendicular to the surface. Above, it is stated that if a blood droplet hits a surface at a 90° angle, it will be circular. That is true. But in order to do angle calculations, the angle of incidence must be expressed with respect to an imaginary line perpendicular to the surface. Thus, a blood droplet falling perpendicular to a surface is said to impact it at a 0° angle (as in the figure).

As an example of how this kind of information might be useful, imagine that a victim was struck several times with a blunt object and that the victim was standing up as the blows were administered. A medium-velocity blood pattern is produced on a wall nearby as a result of the blunt-force trauma. If there are no reliable witnesses to the events, crime scene investigators need to know whether this victim was standing or lying down when the blunt force was administered. The medium-velocity blood pattern on the wall will have numerous droplet stains, and the droplets that produced them will have hit the wall at many different angles. Investigators can select a sample of the droplet stains, measure them, and compute the angles of incidence. Knowing the angles, they can use string, or wire, or some other straight-line device to reconstruct a line of flight for each droplet. In this example, the lines would tend to converge to an area where the victim's head was located during the blunt force administration. Suppose the lines converge to an area about 5.5 feet (1.7 m) off the ground and that the victim is around that height. Investigators then know that the victim was standing up as the blows were administered, and they have thus partially reconstructed the event from the bloodstain-pattern evidence.

A number of recognizable blood patterns tend to be characteristic of certain events or actions. For example, low-velocity patterns that are the result of gravity alone can change if the source or target is moving. Suppose a person is walking while bleeding, and drops of blood are dripping onto the floor. Depending on the speed of movement, the blood drop patterns may indicate the direction of movement. Another example is when an object or hand dragged through a pool of blood, or a bloody object or hand moved along a surface, creating a pattern called a "wipe." If hair or the bristles of a broom or some other similar object produce the blood pattern, it is called a "swipe." If a victim's artery is severed, and that victim can still move a short distance, the heart pumps blood out of the severed artery and onto the ground or floor producing an arterial spurt blood pattern. In blunt-force injury events the object being used to administer the force may be swung in an arclike motion. Some blood from the injured victim adheres to the object, and as the object is swung, the motion forces the blood off the object and onto nearby target surfaces. Because force is involved, this will produce a medium-velocity pattern. The pattern resulting from such swings of a bloody object is characteristic and known as an arc swing pattern, or sometimes a cast off pattern. Following trails of blood drops can help investigators reconstruct the movements of people at scenes. If the source was moving quickly enough to produce droplets that indicate direction, the trail pattern is more informative. Finally, contact patterns, or contact transfer patterns, can be useful. Any object that comes into contact with a wet blood source will have blood transferred to it. Sometimes, the object can leave a pattern of itself in a bloodstain, and it may be possible to tell what the object was just from examining the bloodstain. An example might be a person wearing corduroy pants kneeling in a wet blood pool. Blood will be transferred to the pants, and it will dry to a contact pattern. But the corduroy pattern could also be transferred to the blood on the floor, and the pattern could be retained as the blood dries out. If the corduroys with the bloodstain are available for analysis, and the scene has been properly documented, investigators may be able to figure out that the wearer of the corduroys probably knelt in the blood at a certain place.

Blood patterns are useful for the reconstruction of events, and this kind of reconstruction can be very helpful in an investigation. In some cases DNA typing does not provide the information necessary to figure out the case. If two people are living together and one is killed, investigators may suspect the other person of the crime. If there was bloodshed, the scene is bloody, and the suspect could have bloodstains on his clothing. Investigators seize the clothes, and then by DNA typing determine that the blood on the suspect's clothes is the victim's blood. The suspect may offer an innocent explanation of the stains: He was present at the bloody scene, knelt down to see if the victim was all right, moved the victim to a more comfortable location, and so on. Only analysis of the bloodstain patterns may help establish the truth about his statements in such a case.

At real-life bloody scenes the patterns are usually complicated, and many of the patterns described above may be overlaid and mixed together. Bloodstain pattern interpretation skill takes both training and experience.

Bloodstains should be analyzed by DNA typing to see whose they are before investigators reach any final conclusions. It may not be obvious how many people were at a scene or how many of them were injured or bleeding. A sound reconstruction will include information about whom the bloodstains match (from DNA analysis), along with an analysis of the patterns.

From these simple examples it will be clear that events cannot be reconstructed completely. In fact, reconstructions are usually partial and may reveal only a small piece of information or information about a small aspect of the overall events. Nevertheless, that piece or aspect might be important in solving the case.

5

DNA Typing

Forensic DNA analysis refers to all the steps and procedures used to isolate, quantitate, and prepare DNA for typing, as well as the typing itself. Forensic DNA typing is the process of finding out the type at one or more loci. DNA profiling means the combination of types at several different loci that, taken together, characterize one specimen or one person. Depending on the technique and the number of loci in the profile, a DNA profile might or might not be individual.

PREPARING DNA FOR TYPING FROM BIOLOGICAL EVIDENCE

Before any typing or profiling takes place, analysts have to extract DNA from the biological evidence specimens. The process of getting DNA out of cells is called "isolation" or "extraction." During and after these steps checks have to be done to see how much DNA has been extracted and how much of it is human DNA. The analyst needs this information to decide how much of the DNA to put into the PCR amplification and typing steps.

DNA Extraction

Any biological fluid or tissue that contains nucleated cells can be used as a source of DNA. A nucleated cell is any cell that has a nucleus. In blood the white blood cells have nuclei and therefore have DNA, but the red blood cells do not. The sperm cells contain most of the DNA that is in semen, but there are also some epithelial cells, which contain DNA. Much less DNA is obtained from a comparable quantity of semen that lacks sperm cells. In vaginal swabs and in buccal (inner cheek) swabs the epithelial cells have DNA. Urine has some cells in it but not too many. Sometimes enough DNA can be isolated from urine to enable successful typing, but not always.

All specimens containing nucleated cells are handled pretty much the same way in DNA analysis. The specimen is combined with an enzyme called proteinase K, which hydrolyzes the proteins nonspecifically; that is, it catalyzes the breakdown of cellular protein. Proteinase K also digests cell and nuclear membranes, releasing all the contents of the cell and its nucleus into the solution. The result of this process is called a "digest." Next, it is common to extract DNA from this mixture using a two-phase system of phenol and chloroform. *Two-phase* means that these two liquids do not mix; when combined, they form two separate layers in a test tube. The two phases and the digested specimen solution are then mixed by shaking, and this causes much of the protein to move into the chloroform layer. The chloroform layer is discarded, while the phenol phase, which contains the DNA, is kept. This extraction process may be repeated two or more times.

The DNA is finally isolated from the phenol phase either by precipitation with ethyl alcohol or filtration using a miniconcentrator. DNA is insoluble in ethyl alcohol, so adding it to a DNA-containing solution causes the DNA to fall out of solution. A miniconcentrator is a small filtration device. The filter retains DNA but allows solutions of phenol, buffer, and so forth to pass through. This device can essentially wash the phenol out of the DNA. The DNA is then recovered in a buffer solution in which it is stable. The miniconcentrator procedure is now common in forensic labs.

There are other ways of processing the proteinase-K digests, such as using special columns lined with materials that adsorb DNA under certain conditions, then release it under other conditions. The mechanism of this adsorption involves oppositely charged molecules attracting one another. A positively charged molecule lining the column will bind DNA. By changing the pH of the buffer solution passing through the column, one can alter the net charges on the column molecules and the DNA so that DNA can be released from the column.

DNA Quantitation

Once DNA has been isolated from the biological specimen material, analysts must check to see how much DNA there is, how much of it is human, and how intact or degraded it might be. There are two traditional methods for estimating the total amount of DNA in solution: spectrophotometry and gel methods. A spectrophotometer is an instrument that can tell how much light of a certain wavelength is absorbed by a solution. Both DNA and protein absorb light at the ultraviolet (UV) wavelengths 260 and 280 nanometers, but DNA absorbs more strongly at 260 while protein absorbs more strongly at 280. Measuring the light absorption at both these wavelengths allows an estimate of the total DNA in solution.

Gel methods were discussed in chapter 3. An agarose gel can be run to see how much DNA is in the solution and whether it is degraded. This gel is often called a "minigel" because of its small dimensions, about three by four inches across and about 1/8 inch thick. It can typically hold up to 20 separate specimens. If known quantities of DNA are placed in some of the gel wells as standards, the intensity of fluorescence of those specimens can be compared with that of specimens from unknown sources to estimate the total quantity of DNA. A discrete band of DNA suggests intactness, or absence of degradation. A streaky or spread-out DNA fluorescence suggests degradation. The DNA can get broken up into smaller fragments by chemical reactions and other mechanisms that affect it once it is outside the body. The farther down the gel DNA fragments travel, the smaller they are. The longer the DNA smear is, the more small fragments there are and the more degraded the specimen is. In the "first generation" of DNA typing, using the RFLP method, degraded specimens would often not work, because intact DNA was required. The reasons for this are explained later in this chapter, in the discussion of RFLP. Now, with all typing based on PCR amplification of the desired loci, degradation is a much less serious issue. With PCR methods degraded specimens are often typable.

It is not enough to estimate the total amount of DNA in a specimen. In forensic work it is necessary to estimate the total quantity of *human* DNA. All the typing steps rely on having enough, but not too much, human DNA. How is it possible to have a lot of DNA but only a little bit of human DNA? The answer is that some forensic specimens are heavily contaminated with bacteria and other biological materials. Saliva has bacteria. Vaginal swabs have bacteria. Any biological specimen that does not dry quickly or suffers much environmental exposure can become infected with bacteria. As a result the DNA isolated from these specimens is a mixture of human, bacterial, and other DNA. The human typing methods do not operate on the nonhuman DNA, so the analyst needs to know the amount of human DNA in each specimen. That way the analyst knows how much specimen to use in the next steps of the overall process.

Until very recently the quantity of human DNA in specimens was estimated using a commercially available Southern blot procedure called Quanti-Blot. In the technique the DNA specimens for testing are blotted onto a nylon membrane, using a device designed for the purpose. Depending on which template is placed in the device, the specimens can be transferred to the membrane as round circles or "dots" of DNA (the dot-blot template) or as thick lines of DNA (the slot-blot template). Next the membrane is placed in a solution with a probe for a human-specific sequence on chromosome 17. The probe hybridizes to (base pairs with) its complementary sequence in the DNA specimens. Then the membrane is washed in a way that allows the probe to stay in place. The probe is labeled with a compound called biotin. A color reaction can be set up to detect the biotin and thus turn the dots a blue color.

The results of this reaction are shown in the photograph. One row or column in the test is set up to contain known amounts of human DNA— for example 80, 50, 30, 10, and five nanograms. The intensity of the blue color is proportional to the quantity of human DNA in the specimen. In the figure row A holds known quantities of human DNA. The dot in column 5—the lowest amount of human DNA—is barely visible. Rows B, C, and D have various specimens of DNA isolated from evidence items (B5, C3, C4, C5, and D5 are empty). The quantity of human DNA in the unknown specimens is estimated by comparing color intensity of the evi-

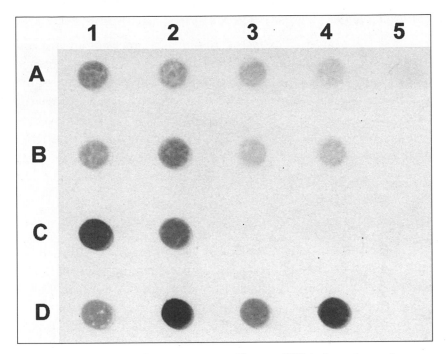

Quanti-Blot membrane for quantitation of human DNA in forensic specimens
(Courtesy of the author)

dence item dots to that of the standards. Item B1, for instance, has about the same quantity of human DNA as is present in the A2 standard. The blue color cannot be seen in the figure, but the intensity of the dots is visible as different shades of gray.

Recently a more complex procedure called real-time PCR (RT-PCR) has come into use for human DNA quantitation. (Unfortunately, the abbreviation *RT-PCR* is also used to mean "reverse transcriptase PCR," and this has nothing to do with real-time PCR. The two should not be confused.) The sidebar "Real-Time PCR" describes the technique. This procedure obviates the need for Quanti-Blot and is more accurate. Use of RT-PCR has also allowed many laboratories to eliminate the minigel step. As long as the quantity of human DNA is determined it is not necessary to estimate the total DNA in a specimen. In addition, DNA degradation is not as important an issue with PCR-based typing techniques, because they will work with very degraded DNA. Accordingly, there is no need to assess degradation in the preparative steps.

THREE GENERATIONS OF DNA TYPING

Once the DNA has been extracted from the specimens of interest and the analyst knows about how much human DNA there is in each one, he or she can proceed to type the DNA. "Typing" is determining either the sequence or the repeat number at a DNA locus in a particular specimen or person. If the specimen or person is typed at several loci, which is nearly always the case, the analyst collects a combination of types called a "DNA profile." As of the early 21st century there have been three generations of forensic DNA tests: RFLP typing, PCR and dot-blot typing, and STR typing.

The First Generation of Technology: RFLP Typing

The original DNA-typing method, first used by Sir Alec Jeffreys in the mid-1980s (as described in chapter 2), was restriction fragment length polymorphism (RFLP). The type of variation in DNA used in RFLP is called "tandem repeat." People are different from one another based on the number of tandem repeats they have at a specific location in DNA (a genetic locus). This polymorphism, or variation among individuals in a population, is called variable number of tandem repeats (VNTR). Within the DNA in the chromosomes are many locations where a DNA sequence is repeated head-to-tail tandemly. A person inherits one member of each chromosome pair from the mother and the other from the father. The numbers of repeats on the maternal and paternal chromosomes can be (and usually are) different.

In the diagram are representations of two people with four different numbers of tandem repeats on their chromosomes at some common location in DNA. Typing consists of isolating or copying DNA from that location, then separating it so the size differences become apparent and can be detected. A size ladder (or sizing ladder) is used to give the analyst an estimate of the sizes of the DNA fragments in the specimens. The ladder is usually made from a virus genome that has been completely sequenced. If this viral DNA is cut with selected restriction enzymes, fragments of known size are produced, and they can be combined to form the ladder. In the figure on page 103, juxtaposed square boxes represent tandem repeats. Each box is a base sequence that is tandemly repeated. M and P represent maternal and paternal. The big box represents an autoradiogram that would result from analyzing these two persons at this DNA locus by

Real-Time PCR

The real-time PCR (RT-PCR) pro-cedure can be used to quanti-tate any DNA for which a unique probe is available and for which PCR primers can be designed to flank the probe-binding region. There are several variations and configurations of RT-PCR. A common one is shown in the accompanying figure.

The procedure is made possible by a probe that has a fluorescent tag at one end and a quencher at the other. A fluo-rescent tag is a molecule that can fluoresce when illuminated with UV light; a quencher is a molecule that can quench, or eliminate, the fluorescence from the fluorescent tag. These molecules are labeled F and Q, respectively, in the figure. PCR primers are added that will flank the probe-binding region. Then the probe binds to one of the DNA strands, the upper strand in the figure. This strand is primed for PCR by the "for-ward" primer in the figure. Next, a DNA polymerase is added to

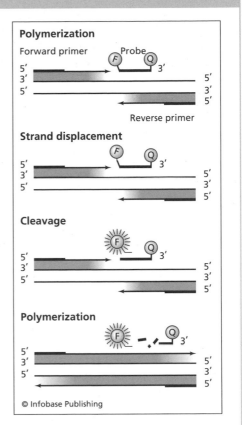

Real-time PCR: In this procedure, PCR is coupled with a probe specific for the DNA region being amplified. A special probe labeled with a fluorescent molecule and a fluorescence quencher is used. The technique is now used in forensic labs to quantitate human DNA.

catalyze copying of the desired segment of DNA. The Taq polymerase enzyme used for PCR has an enzymatic activity called "exonuclease,"

(continues)

(continued)

which under certain conditions allows it to remove bases ahead of the new strand being synthesized. When the PCR reaction reaches the bound probe, the exonuclease activity displaces the bases of the probe. This gets the probe out of the way so that PCR can finish that strand. But it also displaces the F molecule.

As long as the F molecule was near the Q molecule, it could not fluoresce, because Q quenched it. But once it is displaced and free in solution away from Q, it can and does fluoresce. As PCR proceeds, more and more F molecules are displaced, and the fluorescence signal builds up. The fluorescence intensity is proportional to the amount of PCR product formed in the initial phases of PCR, and an RT-PCR instrument can measure the fluorescence and convert this measurement into DNA quantity.

By selecting a DNA region that is human specific, an RT-PCR assay can be designed that quantitates the human DNA in a specimen. Currently, this method is the one used to quantitate human DNA in most forensic laboratories.

the RFLP method. The largest fragment (the one that comes from the piece with the most boxes) moves the slowest and is closest to the top. The smallest fragment migrates fastest and is closest to the bottom. The size ladder would be used to estimate the sizes of the fragments from the people.

Regions of DNA used for forensic identification work were selected partly because many people have inherited different numbers of tandem repeats from their mothers and from their fathers. When the paired chromosomes (the M and the P) differ at the same locus in the same person, that person is said to be heterozygous at that locus. One reason DNA typing is a powerful method of telling people apart is that a large percentage of the population is heterozygous at most of the loci that are used.

The figure on page 104 shows the steps involved in the RFLP procedure, many of which were introduced in earlier sections. RFLP relies on

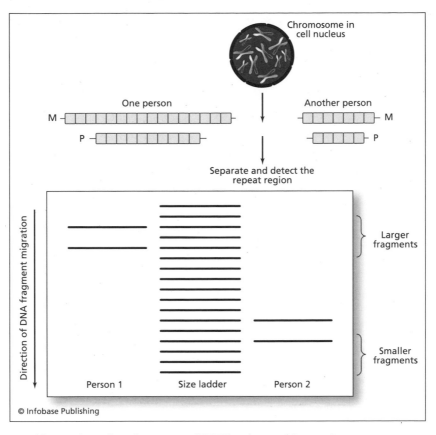

Variable number of tandem repeat (VNTR) polymorphism typing

restriction enzymes, which behave like "molecular scissors," to clip DNA near, but not in, the repeat region. Once the restriction enzyme has cut DNA into thousands of little pieces, there has to be a way to separate out and detect the region of interest and see how many repeats the person has. The method used to separate out the fragments is electrophoresis on a gel, in which the larger DNA fragments move more slowly than the smaller ones. The DNA fragments from the gel are then Southern blotted onto a membrane, and a probe specific for the DNA region of interest, labeled with radioactive phosphorus, is put into contact with the membrane to allow it to bind (hybridize) specifically to the repeat region fragments. The membrane is washed to get rid of all the unbound probe and excess radioactivity, then placed against a piece of X-ray film to allow the

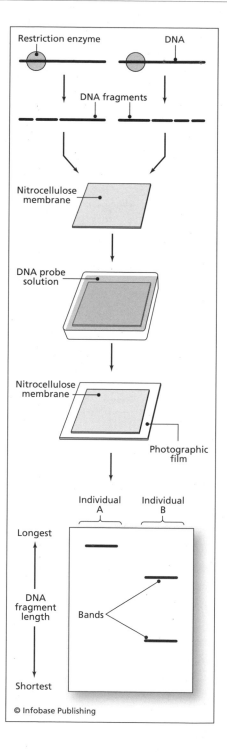

Restriction fragment length polymorphism (RFLP) DNA Typing. In the figure, the membrane for Southern blotting is nitrocellulose; this was later replaced in many labs by nylon membrane. The process illustrated in this figure was used in forensic labs to produce autoradiograms such as the one shown in the next figure.

radioactivity to expose the film. On the developed film, which is called an "autoradiogram," dark bands represent the "bands" where the specific DNA of interest was located.

DNA specimens are initially applied across the width of the gel and migrate from top to bottom. The photograph is an example of an autoradiogram. Each numbered or lettered lane (column) represents a different specimen. *L* means ladder. Ten specimens are represented in the diagram

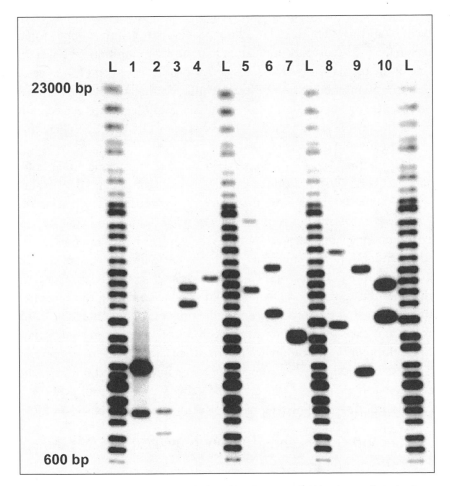

An autoradiogram showing the results of RFLP typing. DNA migrated vertically from top to bottom. Lanes with different specimens are numbered 1 through 10, and sizing ladder lanes are labeled L. The largest ladder fragment is about 23,000 base pairs; the smallest, about 600 base pairs. *(Courtesy of the author)*

along with four ladder lanes. The ladder lanes were interspersed across the gel to increase the accuracy of estimating the size of the DNA fragments from each specimen. Most specimens show two fragments, meaning the person is heterozygous. The largest ladder fragment is about 23,000 base pairs (bp), and the smallest, about 600 bp.

What an analyst really wants to determine is how many repeats a person has at a locus. The problem with RFLP is that it cannot resolve the fragments well enough to tell the actual repeat numbers. RFLP DNA types consist of estimates of the fragment sizes. Even with that limitation the technology proved powerful in telling people apart. If, for example, a person in the U.S. Caucasian population had the most common type at every one of the regularly typed loci, his or her profile would still be expected to occur in only about one of every 40 million unrelated people. In other words, among about 200 million Caucasians in the United States, only about five people are expected to share that same DNA profile. That is not individuality, but it is getting close to it.

Despite this, RFLP technology had some serious disadvantages for forensic work. First, it requires a relatively large sample of DNA to start with, 200 to 300 times more than current methods. Forensic scientists have no control over how much material will be found in evidence that comes into the laboratory, and at times there might not be not enough for RFLP. Second, RFLP requires DNA that is fairly intact—that is, not too degraded. A degraded specimen could consist of fragments smaller than the ones the restriction enzyme would produce, making the specimen untypable using this procedure. But the greatest disadvantage of RFLP is that it is exceedingly labor intensive and slow. It takes an analyst days to get through the procedure for just one locus and weeks to do a profile. There is no good way to automate the procedure or speed it up enough to meet the demands of casework and databanking. As a result RFLP was abandoned in favor of better and faster techniques, those based on PCR.

The Second Generation of Technology: PCR and Dot-Blot Typing

DNA-typing methods that followed RFLP were based on the polymerase chain reaction. Using PCR to make lots of copies of a segment of DNA is called "amplification." Because the segments of interest in DNA are copied multiple times, one can start with a lot less DNA at the front end. Most typing techniques today are optimized for approximately one nanogram of DNA, that is, one-billionth of a gram. Scientists do not know exactly how much DNA there is in a single cell, but there are estimates. One nanogram of DNA represents approximately the amount in 100 cells. So, in an item of biological evidence that has only 100 cells, one could expect to successfully get types based on PCR.

The ability to type DNA in small quantities of biological evidence is clearly an advantage in forensic work. In addition, because PCR can type regions a lot smaller than those used in the RFLP technique, results can often be obtained in degraded specimens. The ability to get types from such small amounts of DNA is very useful, but it also creates some problems and concerns. Those handling biological evidence in the field and in the laboratory must take care to avoid contaminating it with other biological evidence, other biological material, or the handler's own DNA. In the laboratory various precautions are taken to avoid any contamination of evidence specimens or DNA isolated from them.

The second generation of DNA-typing technology consisted of typing a locus called HLA-DQA1, and later five more loci, using dot-blot techniques. Typing was based on amplifying DNA by the PCR, then determining the type or types. The technology was made possible on a large scale by a typing kit designed by scientists at Cetus Corporation and marketed by PerkinElmer. This clever typing kit consisted of strips of nylon membrane to which had been attached DNA probes for specific types at the different loci. First the DNA in the specimens was amplified by PCR, and then the amplified product was placed together with the nylon typing strips, allowing the PCR product to pair up specifically with its complementary probe. A color reaction then turned the positive "dots" on the strip blue. The pattern of dots on the strip allowed the scientist to read the DNA type. The upper part of the accompanying figure shows sample results of "dot-blot" DNA typing.

For several years this dot-blot DNA-typing technology was the only one based on PCR. Some labs would do RFLP where possible and use dot-blot if RFLP did not work, usually because there was not enough specimen or the specimen was too degraded. Other labs used dot-blot typing techniques and never did RFLP. The HLA-DQA1

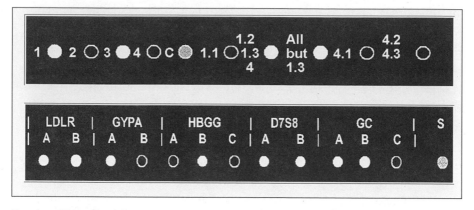

Results of DNA dot-blot typing. The upper image is a diagram of an HLA-DQA1 typing strip. The lower image is a diagram of a PM typing strip. *(Courtesy of the author)*

locus typing strips (shown in the upper part of the figure) were available for several years before the additional five locus strips were (these are called PM, or Polymarker, and are shown in the lower part of the figure).

A drawback of the dot-blot method is that the combined types in DQA1 and PM usually did not have the low probabilities of chance match that were common with RFLP profiles. In other words, the dot-blot typing was not as individualizing as RFLP. In match cases the probability of a chance duplicate profile was usually on the order of one in a few thousand to one in 30,000 to 50,000, or so. Recall that for RFLP typing, even a DNA profile with the most common type at each locus would occur only in about 1 of every 40 million people. Because the dot-blot typing method was based on PCR, however, it could type many specimens that could not be typed by RFLP. The dot-blot method was used in a number of post-conviction DNA exclusions in the late 1980s and early 1990s, in which DNA typing that was not available at the time of a conviction showed later that the person was excluded as the source of biological evidence.

The Current Technology: STR Typing

As described earlier, many loci in human DNA show VNTR polymorphism. Among them are many loci that have short repeat motifs of two to five base pairs. These loci are called short tandem repeats (STRs). They are also sometimes called microsatellites. For technical reasons forensic scientists concentrated on four and five base-pair repeats. The desirability of having DNA fragment detection techniques sensitive enough to distinguish single repeats was an important factor in developing the current technology. In other words, scientists wanted a method that could tell if someone had 10 repeats, or 11 repeats, or 12 repeats at a locus. Since the repeat unit is 4 at some loci, the detection techniques have to be able to distinguish fragments that differ by four base pairs. There are certain gel techniques, commonly used for sequencing, that can do so. Capillary electrophoresis is capable of this resolution as well.

Another big consideration as forensic science moved into this third generation of DNA-typing technology was efficiency, represented by the potential for automation and high-specimen throughput. This is because the story of forensic DNA typing in recent years is mainly a story of backlogs. Specimens come into the laboratory faster than they can be worked on and sent out. But a feature of PCR not previously mentioned, called "multiplexing," had the potential to ease backlogs.

In singleplex PCR a single pair of primers that define a small DNA region is added to make lots of copies of that one region. In multiplexing two or more pairs of primers are used that define two or more loci in the same PCR process. Set up properly, this strategy will produce two or more PCR products—that is, two or more loci will be amplified simultaneously. By optimizing PCR reaction conditions quite a few loci can be simultaneously amplified, or multiplexed. Obviously, this strategy saves a lot of time and effort.

In addition to the ability to amplify several STR loci at once, forensic labs need a fast method to detect and size the PCR products. Capillary electrophoresis, which is just electrophoresis in a small capillary tube, can be used to accomplish this task. Recall that fragments migrate faster if they are smaller and more slowly if they are bigger. It is possible to design PCR so that the products from three different loci are different sizes, because the size of the fragment is controlled by where the primer sites are. If run through the capillary all at once, they would be separated by virtue of their size differences.

The capillary electrophoresis column passes through a detector so that the separated products can be detected and recorded. Detection of the fragments at the end of the capillary is based on laser-induced fluorescence. Carefully chosen dyes, which fluoresce at specific wavelengths when exposed to a laser, can be incorporated into primers. As the fragment passes the laser beam, it is illuminated and fluoresces at the specific wavelength determined by the dye, and the fluoresced light is measured by the detector.

To increase throughput even more this design can go a step further. Suppose six PCR products are put into the capillary at once, three with dye A and the other three with dye B. The three dye A products differ in size, as do the three dye B ones. As the products pass the laser, all six can now be distinguished. By calibrating this system with DNA fragments of varying known size, one can determine the sizes of the fragments and convert that information into numbers of tandem repeats.

In practice there are instruments and STR-typing kits that incorporate all the design features just described. The instruments come equipped with computers and software that translate the instrument readings into useful information about the DNA specimen. Many forensic science laboratories type nine loci with one kit and four other loci with another kit. (The second kit actually has two additional loci that duplicate what is in the first one.) Both have X and Y markers so an analyst can tell if a specimen is male or female.

A person can have 10 or 15 different possible genes (repeat numbers) at every one of these 13 loci. So, the number of possible different combinations is staggering: A 13-locus DNA profile (a list of the types at all 13 loci) in which a person has the most common type at every STR locus has a chance match probability of about one in 166 billion unrelated people in the U.S. Caucasian population. Obviously, there are not that many people in the United States or even in the total world population; this is a probability figure. But because of its magnitude, most people consider such a profile to be effectively individual. That is why the technology is so powerful for individualizing biological evidence.

Because STR-typing technology is so powerful and efficient, it is also in demand, and commercial producers have responded by developing DNA-typing products based on STR. One version of forensic typing kits available today, as just noted, permits profiling of nine and six loci, respectively. The figures on pages 112 and 113 show both a nine-locus DNA profile (from the ABI Profiler Kit) and a six-locus DNA profile (from the ABI COfiler Kit). These two figures depict DNA from different individuals, but in a forensic case the DNA would all be from the same person.

The nine-locus figure shows results for the loci called D3S1358, VWA, FGA, D8S1179, D21S11, D18S51, D5S818, D13S317, and D7S820. The loci are divided into three groups, based on which dye was used to label primers. The left-most result in the second "row" (green dye) is XY, the gender marker; the person in this profile is a male. The figure represents a trace obtained from instrumentation manufactured by ABI. The six-locus figure shows results for the loci called D3S1358, D16S539, THO1, TPOX, CSF1PO, and D7S820. Two of these are replicates of the loci typed by the nine-locus kit, while four are different. The XY result is in the same position on this profile as in the other figure.

Typing using the two kits results in a 13-locus profile and also allows the analyst to tell whether the person is male or female. The 13-locus STR DNA profiling is now the standard in the United States. All case items and databank specimens (databanks are discussed later in the chapter) submitted to laboratories are tested for this same 13-locus profile.

MITOTYPES AND Y-CHROMOSOME MARKERS

Mitochondrial DNA (mtDNA) is present in both males and females and inherited only from one's mother. Y chromosomes are present only in males and are inherited only from one's father. Occasionally, nuclear DNA typing cannot be carried out successfully or is not sufficient on its own. In those situations either conducting mtDNA typing or identifying Y-chromosome markers can sometimes help investigators resolve an identity or a case.

Mitochondrial DNA Typing

As briefly described earlier, the mitochondrial genome is small compared with that of the nucleus, and the segment containing most of the variation of interest to forensic scientists is only a few hundred base pairs in length. Mitochondrial DNA typing is sequencing, as it is the sequence that varies from person to person. But not every base in the sequence varies. Certain positions in the sequence vary a lot more often, and mtDNA typing focuses on those positions. A statement of what bases a person has at those highly variable positions is called a "mitotype." Mitochondria are inherited from one's mother; the mitochondria come from the egg, not the sperm. Unless there have been mutations, an individual's mitotype will be the same as that person's mother, her mother, her mother's mother, and so on.

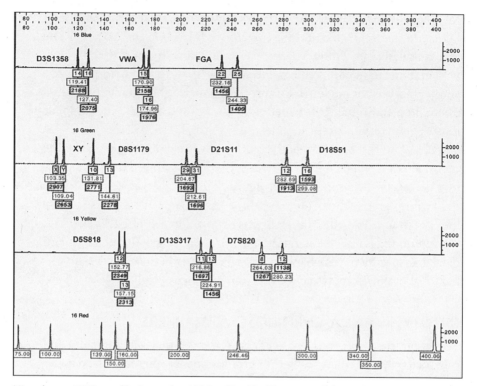

Nine-locus DNA profile from the ABI Profiler Kit *(Courtesy of the author)*

There are many mitochondria in every cell. Thus, there are many copies of mtDNA in every cell, whereas there is only one copy of nuclear DNA in any cell. In old, weathered, degraded biological specimens, mtDNA sequencing has proved its worth in helping identify human remains. The DNA lab responsible for identifying U.S. military remains uses mtDNA for the purpose. Both of its key features—multiple copies and maternal inheritance—contribute to the success of mtDNA in these endeavors. The multiple copies help because even if the specimen is very degraded, there is a chance that a few copies of the desired sequences have survived. Maternal inheritance helps military labs when they are obtaining "reference" specimens for comparison, because only persons in the maternal lineage need to be considered.

There are situations when mtDNA typing is helpful in criminal cases as well. Once in a while nuclear DNA cannot be recovered in sufficient quantity from a specimen. Whereas there is mtDNA in the shafts of a person's hair, for example, there is no nuclear DNA there at all. So, if hair shafts are the only biological evidence, mtDNA typing is the only DNA option available.

Mitotypes are not individual. Depending on the population, the same mitotype occurs in one in every several hundred to one in every several thousand people. Matching mitotypes does not amount to individualization. But if there is other circumstantial evidence in the case, matching mitotypes can be quite convincing. Suppose, for example, the military knows that Captain John Smith was flying a helicopter that crashed in Vietnam in 1967. If decades later skeletal remains are taken from an old, wrecked helicopter in Vietnam that had the same serial numbers as the captain's helicopter, the circumstances lend support to the hypothesis

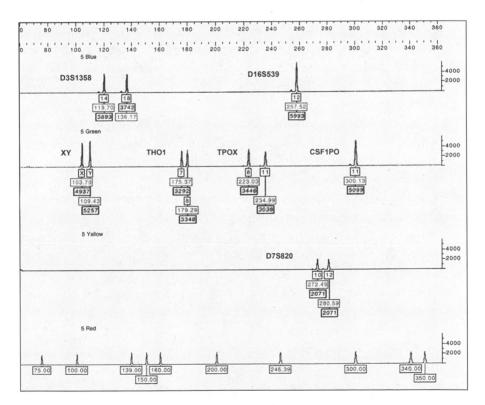

Six-locus DNA profile from ABI COfiler Kit. This profile is from a different person than the one in the previous figure. In a forensic case or a databank specimen, the same specimen or person is profiled for all 13 loci. *(Courtesy of the author)*

that the remains belong to him. At that point reference specimens can be sought and mitotyping done in an attempt to confirm the identity.

Because of the high copy number of mtDNA in specimens, and because specimens are often contaminated with other human biological traces that can have mtDNA, contamination is a more serious problem in mitotyping than in nuclear DNA profiling. Mitochondrial DNA typing is a specialized process. Only a small number of laboratories have mtDNA capability.

Y-Chromosome Markers

Males have Y chromosomes; females do not. The Y chromosome is passed down from father to son in the same way as mtDNA is passed down from mother to child. For quite a while geneticists were not sure the Y chromosome had any functional genes, but recently more has been learned about it. The Y chromosome bestows "maleness" on a child. Males are chromosomally XY. There are several STR regions on the Y chromosome. It is now possible to type them, just as the other STRs mentioned above are typed. But why would anyone want to? There are already enough STR loci to individualize biological evidence. The answer to that question requires some explanation.

Much of the evidence that comes into the forensic science laboratory originates from sexual assault cases. The vaginal swabs and underwear stains are often mixtures of female epithelial cells and male sperm cells. Isolating, or extracting, DNA from the cells in biological evidence was discussed earlier. In mixtures of spermatozoa and epithelial cells, it is possible to extract the DNA from the epithelial cells first, then go back and extract the DNA from the sperm. That way one has separate female and male DNA. The female DNA belongs to the complainant in the sexual assault, while the male DNA belongs to the semen depositor. The male DNA profile can then be compared with that of any suspected depositor. This sequence is called "differential extraction," and in many cases it works fine, but sometimes it does not.

In degraded specimens, cells may already be broken open, and under those circumstances DNA extraction yields mixtures of male and female cell contributions. Another example where differential extraction is not effective is specimens containing semen with no sperm. In this case the male DNA comes only from epithelial cells, and the extraction step again yields a mixture of male and female DNA. Mixture profiles can be hard to interpret, especially when the people share alleles at one or more of the loci. The analyst has to look at the mixture profile and decide if the male could be a contributor, given that the female is a contributor. It is not always clear cut. In addition, it is not always straightforward to calculate the percent of the population who could be contributors in a nonexclusion situation.

Y-chromosome typing helps solve these problems. The profile of markers on one chromosome is called a haplotype. The Y haplotype from a specimen can only come from the male. A forensic scientist can compare it with the haplotypes of suspected depositors without worrying about female-male mixtures. There is, of course, the possibility that more than one male contributed semen. If that is the case, the Y haplotypes will be the result of a mixture.

Y haplotypes can help get around the female-male mixture problem, but they are not individual. Many men will share a haplotype, so other evidence would be required to point to a particular man.

DNA PROFILE DATABASES

One of the things about DNA profiles that is so helpful to law enforcement is the ability to store the profiles and search for them later. DNA profiles can be stored and searched in the same way as latent fingerprint images in the automated fingerprint identification systems (AFIS). Why store DNA profiles? There is a considerable tendency toward recidivism among people who commit crimes; that is, a person who commits a certain type of crime tends to do so over and over again. And there is a small but very dangerous group of individuals who are serial rapists and/or serial killers. If storing DNA profiles helps apprehend these offenders, many people would be in favor of it.

Keep in mind that DNA is not quite the same as fingerprints. The only thing fingerprints can really be used for is to identify a person; indeed, that is the purpose of having the files. But a person's DNA contains a lot of information besides just who that person is. These questions arose early in the era of DNA typing, when the U.S. Congress and state legislatures were first considering DNA databasing laws.

It has been noted that the VNTR variations in DNA that are used to identify people do not have any known function. In other words, doing a forensic DNA profile using VNTRs does not reveal anything about how someone looks, his or her age, whether the person has any illnesses, what race he or she is, and so on. None of those things can be learned from a forensic DNA profile alone. The profile is a kind of numerical code, and the code can be matched to one that is already in a database in order to identify a person.

When database legislation was first being considered, Congress and state legislatures discussed issues of privacy and civil liberties surrounding DNA typing. The law-enforcement community assured Congress that the DNA typing used for identification—the DNA profile—does not provide any information about the person other than identity. Thus, in practice it is not different from a conventional fingerprint.

Lawmakers decided that only the DNA profiles of persons actually convicted of crimes would be placed into searchable files. Each state law specifies which crime convictions result in a person's DNA profile being databased. Some states database only those convicted of felony sexual assault offenses, while others database anyone convicted of a felony. State laws also differ on whether juvenile offenders can be databased.

Since U.S. law-enforcement bodies began to database DNA profiles, the tendency has been for state legislatures to expand the database programs by increasing the range of crimes for which a convicted individual is databased. There have been efforts to change the policy in order to database the DNA profiles of arrestees as well as convicted offenders. A few states have already enacted this change. Another issue is how far back to extend the database program. Most states have databased everyone who was in prison or under correctional supervision for a covered crime at the time the law was passed, as well as all new convicted offenders. The impetus behind expanding the database is this: The more people who are databased, the higher the probability will be of finding a match when searching for a new profile.

Forensic laboratories, or often one lab in a big system, store DNA profiles in computer files. There is one repository for each state. There is also one large national database maintained by the FBI; the system is called CODIS, for Combined DNA Indexing System. There is another file of DNA profiles besides that of the convicted offenders. It is commonly called the "forensic file." These are profiles of as-yet-unidentified perpetrators of unsolved crimes. For instance, suppose a woman was sexually assaulted by a stranger wearing a ski mask, and she never got a look at him. The vaginal swab from her sexual assault examination can yield semen that provides a DNA profile. This is the profile of her assailant, but his identity is unknown. Profiles such as these make up the forensic file. The forensic file can show associations between cases that are not otherwise apparent to investigators. Many large laboratories serving large population centers maintain local databases called LDIS (the L stands for "local"). State databases are called SDIS, and the states upload their data to the national system, called NDIS. So, anyone working anywhere can search (or get the closest authorized person to search) for a profile from a case in either the convicted offender file or the forensic file. If the profile is found in the convicted offender file, the person is identified. If the profile is found in the forensic file, it means his or her profile showed up in another crime.

When a search for a case profile in one of these files finds a match, it is called a "cold hit," and cold hits have now become routine. Numerous cases have been solved using these database files to identify suspects. In large cities forensic laboratories now regularly associate different sexual assault cases with the same offender, even when the police had no previous reason to think the cases were connected. Similarly, the laboratory can dissociate cases the police thought were connected to the same offender. There are rules about who can access these files. They are kept very secure, and there are criminal penalties for unauthorized access to them or unauthorized revelations from them.

A forensic scientist might say "the profile was entered into CODIS." That means it was entered into the database. In order for the database concept to work every laboratory entering profiles into the system has to be typing the same loci, that is, generating the same DNA profile. Database sharing is the reason everyone has to use the same loci for a DNA profile. The value of being able to search for a profile nationally is considered greater than the value of each individual lab being able to pick its own DNA profiling methodology.

The 13 STR loci routinely typed in forensic laboratories are sometimes called the "CODIS core loci," because they were the loci agreed upon by consensus among forensic scientists when STR technology was implemented. Profiles entered into the files must have a minimum number of loci, but they do not necessarily have to have all 13. The reason for choosing the 13 is that the probability of chance duplication among unrelated people greatly exceeds the U.S. population. A 13-locus profile is expected to be unique within the database and thus is associated with a single person. If a smaller number of loci had been chosen, the probability of chance duplication would be greater: When the database reached a certain size there would be duplicates, and investigators would have to spend time and effort sorting out the individuals who shared the smaller profile. To avoid this problem planners decided to include more loci in the profile.

When people discuss the future of DNA typing, the possibility of using a new technology, such as SNPs (discussed later in this chapter), often comes up. But changing to a new standard is problematic, because any switch in technology means that every specimen in every database would have to be reprofiled using the new system. System-wide reprofiling has been undertaken once already: Recall that the databases first had RFLP data in them. After several years, in the late 1990s, the whole system was converted to the STRs. Even then, when there were not very many profiles in the system, it was a huge and expensive task. As of October 2007, according to the FBI, there were more than 5 million convicted offender profiles and more than 194,000 forensic profiles in the national system. Any decision to change technologies must take into account the costs of the conversion along with the benefits of the new system.

Laboratory Backlogs in Processing DNA Cases and Specimens

Despite the successes of DNA profiling technology—and there have been many—there remains a serious problem of backlogs in the forensic laboratories. There are backlogs in cases as well as in developing offender specimens for entry into CODIS. As legislatures have broadened the range of criminal offenses for which a person can be databased, the number of specimens requiring processing has increased proportionately. Backlogs prevent the full and effective use of DNA technology in criminal investigation. The sidebar "DNA Case Backlogs" explores this problem.

APPLICATIONS OF DNA PROFILING

There are three primary forensic applications of DNA profiling: resolving criminal cases, resolving parentage cases, and identifying human remains when conventional methods fail. Criminal cases involve blood or body fluid transfers that happen during some criminal activity. Biological evidence from crimes can be DNA profiled to see whether it matches or fails to match persons involved or suspected of being involved in the case. DNA matches associate people with evidence. They do not by themselves usually prove that anyone committed a crime.

Parentage cases arise when it is necessary to establish legally that a person is the parent of a child, or a child of a parent or parents. Most of the cases are disputed paternity matters, where a man is named by a mother as the father of her child. If he disputes the allegation, DNA testing is done. These cases usually involve child support payments by the biological father, but they can involve other matters such as inheritance of a large estate.

Human remains are generally identified by direct viewing or by fingerprints or dental records. If none of those methods can be used, DNA typing may be done. The DNA profile from human remains might be matched to an item a person owned and used, such as a toothbrush. Or, the profile can be compared with that of parents, children, or other relatives to help establish who the deceased person was.

Resolving Criminal Cases

If blood or other biological evidence is recovered from a crime scene, from a crime victim, or from a victim's clothing or belongings, DNA profiling might help resolve the case. For instance, the DNA recovered from a scene or victim might match someone involved in the case, might not match anyone involved in the case, or might not match anyone involved in the case but might match a profile in the database.

When a DNA profile from crime scene evidence or a victim matches that of a person, the probability of chance duplication is usually extremely small. In other words, there is a very high probability that the recovered DNA belongs to the person. Some blood or body fluid evidence may match the crime victim, but other evidence may implicate a suspect. Matching DNA evidence strongly implicates a person in the crime unless there is an innocent explanation for the biological evidence. In serious assault cases where blood is transferred, a perpetrator may acquire the victim's blood on his clothing. He may claim, however, that he did so while trying to aid the victim rather than during violent events. Similarly, in a sexual assault case, a man who is implicated by biological evidence may state that the

DNA Case Backlogs

In August 2001 U.S. attorney general John Ashcroft directed the National Institute of Justice (NIJ) to make an assessment of the existing delays in processing of DNA specimens in criminal cases and for CODIS. In a March 2003 report to the Attorney General's Office, NIJ estimated that some 350,000 serious criminal cases (sexual assault and murder) were backlogged. About 10 percent of these cases were estimated to be in forensic laboratories awaiting analysis. The remainder was still in the custody of law enforcement; they had not yet been submitted to a forensic laboratory. Asked why they had not submitted the cases, law-enforcement bodies said the primary reason was that the forensic laboratory would not be able to process them in a timely manner.

NIJ made the following six major recommendations to help correct the problems:

1. Improve the DNA analysis capacity of public crime laboratories

2. Help state and local crime labs eliminate casework backlogs

3. Eliminate existing convicted offender DNA backlogs

4. Support training and education for forensic scientists

5. Provide training and education to police officers, prosecutors, defense attorneys, judges, victim service providers, medical personnel, and other criminal justice personnel

6. Support DNA research and development

These recommendations formed a basis for the President's DNA Initiative, a five-year program announced in March 2003 that will make more than $1 billion available to improve efficiency and reduce backlogs in DNA processing for criminal cases and CODIS.

A comprehensive study supported by the Bureau of Justice Statistics (BJS), another government body, collected considerable data on forensic laboratories for the calendar year 2002. It showed that the backlog problem was not limited to DNA cases but was a more general problem in forensic laboratories. The laboratories included in the survey reported about 29,500 backlogged DNA cases as of January 1, 2002. During the year approximately 60,800 new cases were submitted, and around 41,500 were analyzed and sent out, leaving a total backlog at year's end of about 48,800.

One strategy that has been used to help reduce backlogs is outsourcing, sending the work out to another qualified contract laboratory. In the BJS study about 40 percent of the laboratories outsourced work during 2002, and more than 90 percent of the outsourced work was related to DNA cases or CODIS specimens. In the 50 largest forensic laboratories, for every case processed during 2002 there were about 1.75 backlogged cases outstanding at year's end.

Another study designed to assess backlogs as well as the potential for DNA analysis was published in December 2003 by NIJ. Those researchers estimated that more than 221,000 homicide and sexual assault cases with possible biological evidence had not been submitted to a forensic lab by law enforcement for analysis. The comparable number is 264,000 cases of property crime. About 57,000 cases were backlogged in the forensic laboratories surveyed awaiting DNA analysis. The NIJ report suggests that much more benefit can be derived from DNA analysis in criminal cases if appropriate resources become available to clear up backlogs and keep systems current going forward.

In spite of the considerable funds expended through the president's initiative and the accompanying efforts to reduce casework and database backlogs, they have persisted. The addition of offenses for which a person can be data banked, and legislation in some states to include arrestees or suspects in the database program have added to the caseloads. Backlogs will likely be a factor in forensic DNA analysis for some time.

sexual relations were consensual, that there was no assault. DNA profile results must therefore be interpreted in the context of the case.

Sometimes, in a situation where one would expect to find the true perpetrator's DNA profile, the DNA profiles from evidence in a case do not match a suspect. In these circumstances the suspect is excluded. He or she is not the depositor of the biological evidence from which the DNA profile came. There are many cases in which suspects are excluded and freed from suspicion following DNA profiling. There are also unfortunately many cases in which someone has been convicted of a violent offense before DNA profiling was available and is then excluded years later by DNA profiling of the original case evidence. Gary Dotson, discussed in chapter 2 in the sidebar "ABO Blood Typing and Inclusion," was among the first individuals to be exonerated after conviction based on DNA profiling.

When DNA profiles from case evidence do not match a suspect in a case, or when there is no identified suspect in a case, there might be a match to a profile in the database, a CODIS "hit." This match could be to a convicted offender profile, in which circumstance the person is identified, or it could be to a profile in the forensic file, in which case the case is connected to another unsolved case. These CODIS matches can be very helpful to law enforcement. When a database hit connects evidence to a convicted offender, the depositor is identified, and the case is likely solved. In these cases the laboratory does not rely on the database match as the evidence for the case. Rather, a new specimen is taken from the person, profiled, and compared with the evidence profile. When a hit connects evidence to a profile in a forensic file, the case is connected to other unsolved cases, and law enforcement may be able to pool information to help solve the cases.

As the number of profiles in CODIS has grown, the number of matches has grown as well. The table on page 124 shows some of this data through October 2007. The majority of these CODIS matches were found by searches conducted by state laboratories. The data provide a clear illustration of the growing value of the CODIS database in assisting the investigation of criminal cases.

Sometimes nuclear DNA profiling cannot be done in a criminal case, or for some reason it gives no results. In those cases, where there is biological evidence, mtDNA typing may be used. For instance, hairs with no roots cannot be profiled using nuclear DNA but can be mitotyped.

Mitotyping of evidence and people involved in a case can include or exclude people. Exclusions show that the person tested did not deposit the evidence. Inclusions are much less individualizing than they are with nuclear DNA: About one in several thousand people has any given mitotype. Mitotypes have not been databased, however, so there are no files to search for mitotypes that do not match anyone in a case.

Interpretation of DNA Results

There has been considerable media coverage of DNA technology and the dramatic effects it has had in criminal cases. Post-conviction DNA exclusions brought to light a number of initially wrongful convictions, perhaps suggesting that DNA typing is some kind of panacea, a solution to all our criminal justice problems. But DNA inclusion and exclusion are not the equivalent of guilt and innocence. Such a statement as "DNA proved a man innocent" is not correct. DNA cannot by itself prove anyone innocent or guilty. All it can do is include or exclude someone as a depositor of biological evidence. The rest is inference, independent of the DNA results.

DNA profiling and interpreting the results of the laboratory procedures is not always simple and straightforward. There are two levels of interpretation. First is the interpretation of the DNA typing and testing results themselves. Second is the interpretation of what results mean in terms of the case.

Suppose that a woman reports to the police that she was sexually assaulted by a man and that she has a good idea of who the man is. She is examined, specimens are taken, and semen on the vaginal swab is profiled for DNA. It does not match the profile of the suspect, so he is excluded as the donor. Does this mean the woman was raped by someone else? On the face of it, that is what the findings suggest, but there are other possibilities. Perhaps this man really did rape this woman, but he did not deposit semen in her body. Or, perhaps she had a consensual sex partner 48 hours before the incident, but for personal reasons she does not want to reveal this to the police. There can be very different explanations for the same DNA results.

Laboratory analysts sometimes make incorrect judgments about evidence and its analysis. The concept of "best evidence" was described in chapter 4. In sexual assault cases the best evidence is normally the vaginal swab taken from the complainant, but an investigator has to consider the

	2000	2001	2002	2003	2004	2005	2006	2007
Total Offender Profiles	460,365	750,929	1,247,163	1,496,536	2,038,514	2,826,505	3,977,433	5,070,473
Total Forensic Profiles	22,484	27,897	46,177	70,931	93,956	126,315	160,582	194,785
Hits to Offender Database	731	2,371	5,032	8,269	13,855	21,519	32,439	*
Hits to Forensic File	507	1,031	1,832	3,004	5,147	7,071	9,529	*

Source: Federal Bureau of Investigation
* numbers not available as of October 2007

facts of the case in deciding what is the best evidence. A rape investigation that took place in Illinois in the 1990s demonstrates the results of poor judgment about best evidence. In this case a woman reported being sexually assaulted by a man she knew. She had hesitated reporting the incident for a few days, so no sexual assault evidence collection kit was taken. The evidence, which she had preserved, consisted of her clothing. The laboratory focused on the underwear but did not examine the outerwear, even though the victim's statements suggested that there would be more biological evidence on the outerwear. The laboratory's analysis of the underwear gave ambiguous results, primarily because this item had almost no semen. Later examination showed that there was a semen stain on the outerwear, and the DNA profile of this stain did match that of the accused man. It took a lot of extra time and required analysis by other experts and laboratories to eventually sort out this case. If the lab had done this analysis initially, all the interpretive problems could have been avoided.

Parentage and Affiliation Cases

Resolving parentage cases is the second major application of forensic DNA profiling. As noted in chapter 1, parentage cases are usually filed in family courts and usually involve disputed paternity. Society has an interest in ensuring, through its family courts, that minors are financially supported. Paternity tests are ordered to help the court establish a child's true father and then to hold him responsible for that child's support.

Most paternity cases are straightforward, and they often involve testing three people: a mother, her child, and a putative father. *Putative* means that he has been named by the mother as the child's father, but that he denies paternity or is uncertain of it. DNA profiling of the three people can answer the question almost conclusively. Profiling the mother and child enables an analyst to determine which genes the child inherited from its mother. The other gene at each of the loci has to have come from the biological father. These are sometimes called the obligatory genes. If the man tested has them, he is included as a possible father.

Using the known population distributions of the genes at each of the loci, the analyst can calculate a probability of paternity, a probability that this tested man is the child's father versus any other man in the population. In a DNA inclusion test this probability is typically high. The standard of proof in family court is called "preponderance of the evidence." A high probability of paternity calculated from DNA profiling is generally sufficient to establish paternity to the court's satisfaction for purposes of ordering support. If, based on his profile, the man tested in a case cannot furnish the obligatory genes, he is excluded. A man excluded by DNA profiling is absolutely not the father of the child.

In 2007 an interesting but extremely unusual case came to light from New Madrid County, Missouri. Holly Marie Adams had engaged in sexual relations with each of two brothers who were identical twins within the same short period during which her daughter was conceived. The brothers, Raymon and Richard Miller, wanted DNA profiling to establish which of them was the true father. In this unusual case it could not be done. Because they were identical twins, their DNA was identical. Identical twins are the result of a single fertilized egg dividing into two cells, each of which then goes on to develop into a baby. In this case the judge, having ruled that only one man would pay support, had to make an arbitrary decision about which one it would be. There was no scientific way to find out the answer.

Often, disputed parentage cases involve parents and an infant child, but not always. In a case reported by Professor Li Li from the Shanghai, China, Institute of Forensic Science in 2007, a disputed parentage case arose in a family where the child was already a teenager. ABO blood typing had been performed for medical reasons and indicated that this child might not be the child of the parents. DNA typing was performed, and the results are shown in the table on page 127.

Earlier in the chapter DNA loci were discussed, and it was noted that forensic DNA profiling typically uses 13 of them—the CODIS core loci. These loci each have names, and 10 of them are shown in the lefthand column of this table. At each locus a person can have two genes. The genes at each locus are usually numbered. The case can be understood looking at the table without knowing anything more about these locus names and numbered genes. In this table the mother is type 16,17 at the D3S1358 locus, type 16,18 at the VWA locus, and so forth, reading down the second column. This table shows results at 10 loci; in the actual case more loci were typed. The father is excluded from being the son's biological father at several of the loci because the son has genes that the father lacks. For example, at the first locus listed, D3S1358, the son is 16,16, but the father has no 16 gene. The mother is also excluded at several loci. For example, at the locus FGA, the son is 19,23, and the mother has neither of those genes.

So, these are not the biological parents of this child. After the DNA typing was done investigation showed that this child had been wrongly identified as these parents' child in the hospital shortly after he was born.

Identification of Human Remains

Identifying human remains is the third major application of DNA profiling. Both nuclear DNA profiling and mtDNA typing may be used for this purpose. DNA typing should be seen as a last resort method for the identification of human remain when the other, easier conventional methods of identification have failed.

The coroner or medical examiner is usually responsible for identifying deceased persons. Most of the time bodies are identified by having a living person who knew the deceased make a visual identification by viewing the decedent's face directly or by viewing a video or photographic image of the face. Sometimes, though, visual identification is not possible. There may be damage to the face or to the whole body, such as from a fire or explosion or from an automobile, train, or airplane accident. Other times no one can be located who knew the deceased, even if the body is intact.

Authorities then turn to fingerprints and to dental X-rays. If there is a suspected identity (the authorities think they know who it is), the body's

Locus	Mother	Son	Father
D3S1358	16,17	16,16	15,15
VWA	16,18	18,19	16,17
FGA	22,24	19,23	20,25
D8S1179	12,14	12,14	11,13
D21S11	29,31.2	29,31.2	28,30
D18S51	13,22	19,20	16,19
D13S317	20,24	17,20	19,19
D7S820	8,11	10,12	8,10
D16S539	9,11	10,12	9,13
D19S433	14,14	13,15.2	14.2,15

fingerprints can be compared with known prints, if they are in a file some-where. If not, an AFIS search (of computerized fingerprint files) can be tried, but nothing will be found unless the dead person's prints were in the files. There is no central file of dental records. To use them for identification someone has to compare the postmortem records with premortem records, but first authorities have to obtain the records, and this involves establishing one or more suspected identities and locating each one's premortem dental records. If fingerprints and dental records cannot be used or fail to reveal the person's identity, other less direct methods must be used. With skeletal (bones-only) remains forensic anthropologists can provide what is called class information (age, race, stature, gender, and so forth) but not identity. In mass disaster situations clothing or belongings may help. A ring on a finger, for example, might be engraved, or someone might be able to recognize it. Clothing or other jewelry or tattoos could be recognizable by someone who knew the person in life.

If all these methods fail DNA typing may be used. It is the method of last resort because it is costly and time consuming and does not always work. Identification of someone through DNA typing requires specimens from personal items or specimens from relatives. There might be enough cellular residue from the mouth on someone's toothbrush, for example, to get a DNA profile. That profile could then be compared with the DNA profile obtained from a tissue recovered from the dead body. Another approach to DNA identification in these cases is using affiliations and comparing the profiles of relatives. In mass disasters persons related to those who were lost are often asked to provide known specimens (usually buccal swabs) for DNA comparisons. DNA from parents, children, siblings, grandparents, and even relatives further removed could be useful in identifying human remains by DNA typing.

The most challenging recent example of the need to identify human remains in a mass disaster was the World Trade Center destruction by terrorists on September 11, 2001. The New York medical examiner's office is committed to trying to identify all the recovered remains, and they number in the tens of thousands. There was so much destruction that there are thousands of little pieces of flesh, tissue, and bone in the tons of debris from the buildings. About 1,650 people had been identified as of late 2007.

The U.S. Armed Forces place great value on recovering the remains of military personnel killed in service and identifying them. In large regions that were the theaters of past wars—those of the U.S. Civil War, World War I, World War II, the Korean War, and the Vietnam War—remains can be and still are recovered years or decades after the end of the conflict. These are skeletal remains, and there are military laboratories devoted to identifying them.

One such lab is the Joint POW/MIA Accounting Command (JPAC) Central Identification Laboratory in Honolulu, Hawaii (until October 2003 called the Central Identification Laboratory Hawaii, or CILHI). JPAC receives and sometimes goes out and recovers skeletal remains of U.S. military personnel. Its primary expertise is in forensic anthropology and dentistry. The branches of military keep good records of who was assigned where, and there are also good premortem dental and fingerprint records of military personnel. Using that information, JPAC tries to positively identify all recovered remains so that they can be returned to the dead person's family and laid to rest. Another laboratory that the armed forces use for this purpose is that of the Armed Forces Medical Examiner within the Armed Forces Institute of Pathology (AFIP) in Washington, D.C. AFIP has established a DNA identification laboratory called the Armed Forces DNA Identification Laboratory (AFDIL), which uses DNA-typing methods to help identify skeletal remains. These laboratories have helped identify thousands of remains of American military personnel. In 2003 and 2004 two of America's unknown soldiers were identified (see sidebar "Identification of the Unknown Soldiers").

Anthropological, dental, and DNA typing methods have also been used to identify remains from mass graves in places where there was military conflict or where military or paramilitary forces killed civilians. An example is in the former Yugoslavia. Forensic identification techniques have also been used to identify or help confirm the identity of historical figures and suspected war criminals such as Martin Bormann and Josef Mengele from the World War II era.

Using DNA profiles from relatives to establish the identity of human remains is a kind of parentage or affiliation testing. In this arena many different relationships are possible between the relatives who provide reference standards and the decedent. In conventional parentage testing most cases involve a mother, a child, and a putative father. Once in a while there is a case involving disputed maternity, such as when a woman abandons a newborn and the authorities want to locate the mother and establish that she is the real mother.

With skeletal remains mtDNA is usually used as the method of choice for identifying remains by DNA. As noted, mtDNA is maternally inherited, and the reference specimen has to come from someone in the maternal lineage. The matching mitotype alone is not sufficiently individual to make an identification, but when other circumstantial information is concordant with the suspected identity, a conclusive identification can be made.

Identification of the Unknown Soldiers

Many military personnel are buried at the Arlington National Cemetery, across the Potomac River from Washington, D.C. At the time of World War I a special tomb was established for an unidentified soldier from that war. It came to be called the Tomb of the Unknowns, and a special army unit ceremonially guards the tomb at all times. An unknown soldier from World War II, the Korean conflict, and the Vietnam War was each buried in the tomb. A simple inscription on the marble reads: "Here Rests in Honored Glory an American Soldier Known but to God."

In 2003 forensic scientists at the Central Identification Laboratory Hawaii were able to identify the Korean War unknown soldier as U.S. Marine private first class Ronald Lilledahl of Minneapolis, believed to have been killed November 28, 1950. The scientists used an improved procedure for matching dental records to make the identification. In 2004 forensic scientists at the Armed Forces DNA Identification Laboratory using mtDNA were able to identify the Vietnam War unknown as U.S. Air Force lieutenant Michael Blassie of St. Louis, Missouri. He died May 11, 1972. These two soldiers' remains were returned to their families. With modern forensic identification methods, it is unlikely that there will be any more "unknown soldiers" of future wars.

A PEEK INTO THE FUTURE: SNPS

At many locations in the human genome there are single base differences between people. At some location, for instance, one person may have G, while another person has A. This variation is known as single nucleotide polymorphism (SNP). The variation at these SNP locations is binary; that is, in a given person it is either one base or another—there are two possibilities. If it were determined what base was present at one, two, or three of these, it would not help narrow down the number of people with the profile very much. But if 40, 50, 80, or 100 locations could be done quickly and efficiently, the resulting profile would be highly individual. With 30 SNPs, there are around a billion combinations. One could easily calculate how many SNPs it would take to individualize effectively biological evidence.

A newer technology, informally known as "DNA chips," may enable one to determine which base is present at many different locations quickly and efficiently. Specific DNA probes can be attached in some known order to the surface of glass, silicon, and so forth in what is called a "DNA microarray." These probes would then bind to amplified DNA fragments placed with the chip if the sequences were complementary. Using fluorescence or some other suitable detection method, an analyst could quickly determine which probes bound and which did not. In the SNP context a simple microarray could rapidly provide a multi-SNP profile.

While this new technology is tantalizing, it is important to remember that any decision to switch typing and/or profiling technologies would require all the existing databases to be reconstructed using the new format. Another problem with SNPs in forensic DNA typing is that many specimens are mixtures; that is, they have DNA from more than one person in them. An SNP profile would present difficult interpretation problems in mixture specimens.

6

Bugs and Plants

In the first chapter it was noted that this book discussed three forensic specialties: blood and body fluid evidence and its genetic typing, forensic entomology, and forensic botany. This chapter is about forensic entomology, the use of insect life cycles to reconstruct time of death, and forensic botany, the use of plant parts and materials to help resolve forensic cases.

FORENSIC ENTOMOLOGY

Entomology is the branch of biological science that studies insect species. There are millions of insect species, and insects are among the best-adapted groups of living organisms on Earth. Human interaction with insect species takes place in several different ways. Some insects are considered nuisances, undesirable to have around, so people try to find ways to keep them away. Some bite or sting people, while others carry diseases. Still others are agricultural pests; they infest crop or ornamental plants. A few insects will lay their eggs on freshly dead animals (including humans), and a few others infest and feed on carrion. Insects in these last groups are the ones of interest to forensic entomologists.

Insect Life Cycles

Although there is considerable diversity among the insects, they are classified together because they have many things in common. One of these is their life cycle. There are standard stages of the life cycle that are seen in every insect. Eggs, larvae, and puparia are universal. All insects have life cycles similar to the one in the figure, which shows the life cycle of a housefly in simplified form.

Larvae (also known as maggots) hatch from eggs. The maggots are small, wormlike creatures that spend most of this portion of their life cycle feeding ravenously and growing rapidly. The flies that most often colonize human carrion will have three larval stages, or instars, all of which develop in a known and orderly progression. This contrasts with the beetles, which can regulate how many instars they will have due to stresses during their life cycle. If they are underfed or overcrowded, they will reduce the number of larval life stages to increase their ability to survive. Both insect groups, the beetles and flies, will complete the larval stages and find a protected area to form their pupa (with the flies it is known as the puparium). In common language a pupa may be called a "cocoon." After a while a new adult emerges from the puparium, completing the cycle.

The cycle is important because it is predictable. At a given temperature each stage of a particular insect's life cycle takes a specific amount of time, and that time is known to entomologists from their studies. By understanding the life cycles of the carrion insects, a forensic entomologist can accurately add up the lengths of time each of the carrion species takes to grow, given known temperature information. With this knowledge he or she can then accurately estimate how long a deceased person has been dead. Carrion insects will lay eggs on a body as soon as they can. Insects will visit a body that is outdoors very shortly after death. The insects may not have access to a body that is indoors, or their access might be delayed.

Influence of Light, Dark, and Temperature on Insect Life Cycles

Although the insect life-cycle stages are precise, they are temperature dependent. The base temperature is the temperature at or below which the insects will not grow. In addition, the adult insects are inactive during

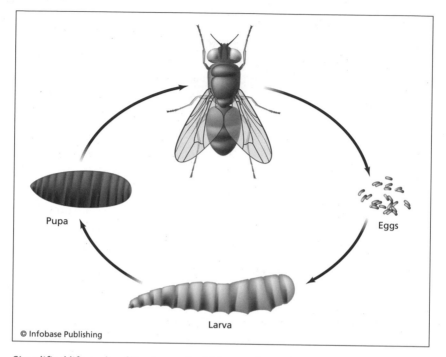

© Infobase Publishing

Simplified life cycle of the housefly. All insects have this type of a life cycle: egg, larva, pupa, adult. In some insects there is more than one larval stage.

hours of darkness (though eggs and larvae will continue to develop during darkness).

Obviously, the temperature changes over time. If there were an accurate recording thermometer at every scene where insect evidence is collected, the entomologist's task would be simpler. Entomologists use the concept of degree-days (or degree-hours) to try to standardize the temperature parameter. Scientists always quote temperatures in degrees celsius. In celsius water freezes at 0°, comfortable room temperature is around 21°, body temperature is 37°, and water boils at 100°. (These same temperatures given in Fahrenheit are 32°, 69.8°, 98.6°, and 212°, respectively.) Entomologists sometimes use the average daily temperature, or they may use the hourly temperature if it is available from a weather station.

In degree-days one day that has an average temperature of 18°C would have eight degree-days when using a base temperature of 10°C. To calculate degree-days or degree-hours the entomologist uses a base temperature. When any temperature is below this base it must be given a value of zero. (Calculations that used negative numbers would show the insect becoming younger, an event does not happen in nature.) Consider an example in which day 1 had a temperature of 20°C, day 2 had a temperature of 25°C, and the base temperature was 10°C. To calculate degree-days the entomologist would subtract the base temperature from the temperature of each day (20–10 = 10 and 25–10 = 15), then add the results (10 + 15 = 25). In this example the result is 25 degree-days. There are data that relate accumulated degree-days to the stage of the insect's life cycle. The entomologist determines the life cycle stage of the oldest insect associated with the body and can then work backward to the time the eggs were laid using degree-days.

Using Insect Life Cycle Stage to Estimate Time since Death

Discovery of a body establishes a point in time at which the person is definitely dead. Investigators next try to determine the time the person was last seen alive. Death had to occur within that interval.

Entomologists are interested in the insect life stages that have been on the body the longest. These creatures have to be identified. Adult insects may be identifiable to an experienced entomologist, but eggs and larvae may not be. For this reason entomologists usually collect those stages alive, bring them back the lab, and rear them to the adult stage. In this way they determine precisely what insect it was and precisely how long it took to develop from whatever its stage was at discovery to adulthood under controlled conditions.

Next, the entomologist collects temperature data from the weather station closest to the site where the body was found. Weather stations are located some distance from one another, and this may create some uncertainty in the calculations of postmortem interval. Accordingly, forensic entomologists have developed statistical methods to help correlate weather station data to conditions at a death scene. One such method is recording the temperature at the death scene for a week or more after the discovery of the body. The entomologist can then compare these data with that from the closest weather station to determine the variance and apply this empirically determined variance to the weather station data for the time period of interest—the time period when the body was actually there. Using this empirically determined "correction" does not prove what the temperatures at the death scene actually were, but it provides an empirical basis for estimating them more accurately.

The number of accumulated degree-days (the sum of elapsed degree-days) for a particular insect to reach a stage in its life cycle is known to entomologists. Accordingly, a forensic entomologist looks first for the oldest insect stage at the death scene—the one that has been present the longest. Having identified the species of that insect, the entomologist back calculates degree-days to find out when the eggs were laid. This calculation may not be exactly the time of death, but it represents the minimum time interval between the laying of the eggs and the collection of the insect evidence at the death scene. Forensic entomologists will perform this analysis not only with the most mature life-cycle stage present but with as many insect species as possible. When calculations from several different insect species arrive at a similar estimate for when the eggs were laid, it gives greater confidence in the estimate.

The value a forensic entomologist's work can bring to criminal investigation and prosecution is illustrated by the Erich Seebeck case, presented in the accompanying sidebar on page 138. The entomologist was able to establish that the death likely occurred when the defendants, who fled immediately after the crime, were still in the area (and thus able to have committed the crime).

The particular insects that will dominate in a body lying out of doors depend on the geographical latitude. Different species are characteristic of northerly versus southern climates. In U.S. latitudes flies usually arrive first, specifically blowflies. The species that may be available to colonize a body in a northern state (such as Wisconsin, Montana, or Maine), most often will be different than those insect species that will be found to colonize a body in southern states (such as Florida, Mississippi, Texas, or southern California).

The blowflies usually begin laying eggs on a decomposing body first. They are a group of about 90 fly species in North America. As decomposition progresses, other groups of insects, mainly other flies and various species of beetles, will come in at known intervals over the course of the process. This phenomenon is known as insect succession, and it is an important concept in forensic entomology. As species of insects colonize the body, they change the biochemistry of the remains. These changes make the body attractive to other species, which then follow.

In many forensic entomology cases the flies are important because they generally arrive first. Later, once the flesh has been removed and the remains have dried out, beetles may start to move in, and they become important.

Forensic entomology is probably used most often to solve violent crimes that leave a victim's body subject to insect colonization, but sometimes, entomological evidence can be helpful in reconstructing events in nonviolent incidents and cases as well. The sidebar "Two Elderly Women in Indiana" on page 140 presents an example of such a case, summarized from a write-up by forensic entomologist and retired FBI special agent Wayne Lord in *Entomology and Death: A Procedural Guide* (1990).

Other Uses of Entomological Evidence

Use of insect evidence to estimate the postmortem interval may be the most frequent way that entomological evidence is used in criminal investigations, but it is not the only one. Insect bites inflicted by chiggers or cockroaches have proved important in certain cases.

Larvae can be used for toxicological analysis, too. As noted, the larvae of certain species readily feed on dead human bodies. In that process they ingest any drugs or toxins that were present in that body. Medical examiners regularly submit blood and other fluids or organs for toxicology testing before they decide on cause and manner of death. With severely decomposed bodies conventional specimens may not be available, but maggots may be. Showing that the maggots feeding on a body contained detectable quantities of cocaine metabolite, for example, establishes that the decedent had used cocaine some time in the past. This information may be helpful in figuring out the reason for the death.

Sometimes, entomological evidence combined with other evidence can help establish both time and location information. In another write-up in *Entomology and Death: A Procedural Guide,* Lord described a sexual assault case where this was the situation. In this case a woman was brutally attacked in an isolated area of a Chicago suburb by a man wearing a ski mask. The police developed a suspect in the case and obtained a search warrant for his apartment. In it they found a ski mask similar to the one described by the victim. The suspect said it was his ski mask but stated that he had not worn it since the previous winter. On the ski mask were cockleburs (a type of seedpod), and they were sent to a forensic entomologist for examination.

The forensic entomologist found small caterpillars inside the cockleburs. This caterpillar belonged to a moth species that had a one-year life cycle. Adults were active in the spring and laid eggs in the early summer. The larvae (caterpillars) develop within the cocklebur in mid-to-late summer, undergo pupation during fall, and then emerge as adults in spring. The entomologist concluded that the ski mask had been outside in mid-to-late summer; that was the only way it could have acquired the

The Erich Seebeck Case

This case is summarized from the write-up of *Erich Seebeck v. State of Connecticut* by the Connecticut Supreme Court (SC 15822, 246 Conn. 514; 717 A.2d 1161; 1998) in ruling on the appeal by Seebeck.

On Friday, June 20, 1980, a 70-year-old man named Ponte Patterson was brutally assaulted and murdered near his home in Waterford, Connecticut, and his car was taken. The two men ultimately convicted of this crime, Erich Seebeck and Adam John, apparently headed west in the stolen vehicle. The same day New York State police found the vehicle abandoned in Brewster, New York, on the westbound side of I-84, about a two-and-a-half hour drive from Waterford. The vehicle had not been reported stolen. Both defendants' fingerprints were in the vehicle. On June 21 one of the defendants called his parents from Pennsylvania. On the afternoon of Tuesday, June 24, a man driving west along the Ohio turnpike picked up the two defendants hitchhiking near Sandusky and drove them to Andalusia, Illinois.

Patterson, the victim, was not discovered until June 24. Once the victim's body was discovered and the investigation began, suspicion quickly focused on Seebeck and John, and they were returned to Connecticut to face charges. Defendant Seebeck had told a witness the day before the crime that he could "get a car from a 70-year-old queer in Waterford." The defendants had also visited Seebeck's parents, whom Seebeck rarely saw, on the Friday afternoon that Patter-

cockleburs with the caterpillars inside. This was the same time when the sexual assault had occurred. Moreover, the cockleburs were similar to ones that were found at the scene during that same time of year. The combination of entomological and botanical evidence in this case was consistent with the ski mask (and, thus, presumably its owner) having been at the scene and having been there at the same time that the assault was perpetrated.

There are not many forensic entomologists available, and a large number of investigators have never received any training in the recognition or

son was murdered, and the parents had seen the men drive away in the stolen vehicle.

The victim's body was discovered by two cousins, who called police. There were indications of a struggle, and the body appeared to have been dragged to where it was found. His right front pocket, where he normally kept his car keys, was inside out and empty. The victim had suffered extensive injuries and had died from a depressed skull fracture probably administered by a brick.

There was considerable maggot activity on the body. The state medical examiners said that the man appeared to have been dead for two to four days. Forensic entomologist Dr. Wayne Lord, who was also an FBI special agent, examined the entomological evidence in this case and calculated that the victim had most likely died in the late morning or early afternoon of June 20. The defense in the case tried to suggest that the defendants had in fact left the state by the time the murder occurred and that the estimates that had them still in Connecticut at the time of the crime were not correct. In other words defense counsel disagreed with the forensic entomologist's conclusions. The alleged uncertainty in the estimation of time of death also provided the basis for appeals from the defendants; however, the Connecticut Supreme Court did not buy these arguments and ultimately upheld the convictions (dismissed the appeal) in 1998.

collection of this sort of evidence. There is not much doubt that entomological evidence is underutilized in investigations. At the same time not every case will have entomological evidence.

FORENSIC BOTANY

Forensic botany could include any type of plant material that had evidentiary value in an investigation. A common application of botanical evidence is the use of cystolithic hairs on the leaf of the marijuana plant as a means of identifying marijuana. Drug identification specialists in forensic labs are taught how to do this, because marijuana is very common as seized drug evidence.

For the most part, however, botanical evidence is not common in criminal or civil cases. There may be several reasons for this. One is that

Two Elderly Women in Indiana

In November 1987 neighbors and acquaintances of a 69-year-old man asked the police to check on him, as he had not been seen for two days. He lived in an affluent neighborhood in a large city in Indiana. The police found the man dead on the living room floor of his home. There were no indications of foul play, and following an autopsy the medical examiner ruled the death as the result of natural causes.

Neighbors had also told police that two elderly ladies, an aunt and a sister of the decedent, were living in the house. According to neighbors, the women were bedridden invalids whom the man was caring for. He regularly indicated his concern about them and their welfare.

Upon further searching the house, police found mummified remains of the two women in their bedrooms. One corpse was in a bed, covered by clothing and bedding. She had been somewhat skeletonized by insect feeding activity (mainly the head and upper torso areas). Several hundred empty blowfly puparia were discovered. The second woman's body was also in bed, but in a bedroom at the opposite end of the house. Though mummified, her remains showed very little skeletonization. Only two blowfly puparia were found at this second location. A substance that the forensic entomologist could identify as fecal material

not many people working in forensic science labs have detailed familiarity with botanical evidence. As a result it is not very easy to have botanical evidence examined. Most investigators are likewise probably not well informed about the potential value of botanical evidence or about collecting and preserving it.

Plant Materials as "Trace and Transfer" Evidence

On those occasions when plant evidence is recognized in an investigation, it will usually be as "trace and transfer" evidence. The term *trace* refers to all sorts of materials, including botanicals that may come up in investigations. It is not a good term because it suggests a small quantity, and that does not have to be the case. The *transfer* concept is the more important. The transfer of the material—in this case, the botanical material—from a source to a target is used as a means of associating the two. (In the

from the beetle *Dermestes lardarius* was also seen in the vicinity of this second body.

The women had been dead for a long time—for years. The forensic entomologist could not tell what year the deaths had occurred, but the entomological evidence permitted him to figure out in what season of the year the deaths had occurred. The first woman probably died in the fall (October), while the second was thought to have died in December or January. Other evidence at the scene confirmed these estimates. The first woman kept a diary, and its last entry was October 5, 1977. The second woman had opened her 1977 Christmas cards, but not her birthday or Easter cards from 1978.

Criminal involvement in either of the women's deaths did not appear likely from the evidence; however, the man had been collecting and cashing the retirement and Social Security checks of the women over the 10-year period. He had collected around $140,000. The retirement fund and the Social Security Administration wanted the unauthorized funds repaid from the estate. In this case the entomological evidence helped establish what the documentary evidence showed, and investigators could be more confident that they knew what had happened.

context of trace and transfer evidence, a "target" is simply the location where a transferred item ends up.) Finding certain botanical evidence on a person's clothing or in or on a vehicle might permit an expert to conclude that the person or vehicle had been in a certain geographical area, because the evidence was specific to that area.

The value of the association that can be made will depend on what the evidence is, how large a geographical area it normally occupies, how it is dispersed by the plant, and so forth. Plant materials of value can be large, such as leaves or seedpods, or microscopic, such as pollen. The study of pollens is called "palynology." Pollens tend to be structurally diverse and resistant to destruction. Pollens from an evidence item can have great potential value.

In the figure on page 143 the small divisions seen in each of the photomicrographs correspond to 2.5 micrometers (a micrometer is one-millionth of a meter, or one-thousandth of a millimeter). The two upper photos are both grains of pine pollen shown in opposing orthogonal (perpendicular) views. There are many species of pine trees, and the pollen from these many species cannot be distinguished well under light microscopy, diminishing their potential use as trace evidence. Furthermore, pine trees are pollinated by wind and are prolific pollen producers. The two "Mickey Mouse ears" visible in the photograph are called "bladders." They are air filled and are responsible for pine pollen traveling long distances by wind. This also decreases the significance of grains of pine pollen in most casework, as their presence does not indicate close proximity to the pollen source.

In contrast, the two pollen grains shown in the lower photomicrographs can have much greater significance. The grain on the left is from the species *Ephedra nevadensis* (Mormon tea). It is specific for that species, and although *Ephedra* is wind pollinated, it degrades more rapidly and travels shorter distances than pine pollen. The pollen grain on the lower right is *Sphaeralcea* (globe mallow). Although specific only to the genus level, this pollen is spread by direct contact (that is, insect pollinated) and is not normally airborne. Many insect-pollinated plants have pollen with highly textured or spiny surfaces to enhance physical adhesion. Based on the presence of this pollen, one can conclude that the jacket has had physical contact with the globe mallow plant, either directly or through an intermediate transfer.

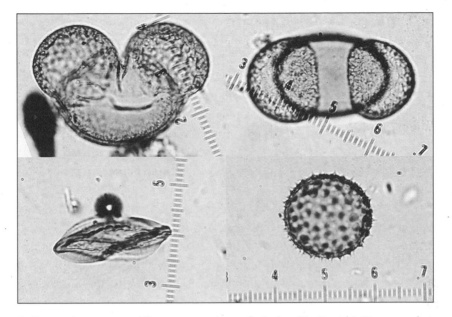

Pollen grains recovered from vacuumings of a jacket *(Dr. David A. Stoney and the McCrone Research Institute, Chicago, Illinois)*

Botanical materials do not have to be land based to be of value. Forensic scientists have occasionally used algae, which live in water, to make associations between clothing and locations. Pathologists, who must diagnose drowning cases, also have an interest in water-based plant life. Diatoms are especially robust and diverse forms of algae that may be found in the lungs of drowning victims.

Botanical analysis does not come up very often in cases, but when it does it can make a valuable contribution to the investigation. For example, a team of botanical (and some other) experts helped sort out a civil case involving the crash of a small airplane in December 1989. This private plane crashed while attempting to land at a small airport in Ruidoso, New Mexico. The pilot and his passenger (his wife) were killed. He was inexperienced, and the weather was bad. The wreckage was gathered and eventually placed in an outdoor storage yard near the airport.

A civil case resulted from this incident. The civil action named as defendants the aircraft manufacturer, the engine manufacturer, and a company that had supplied the fuel control units. The plaintiffs alleged that a part of the fuel supply system had somehow taken in debris and become clogged during flight, thus reducing fuel supply to the engine. The engines were sent back their manufacturer, and the analysis of this debris was at the heart of the forensic investigation that followed.

The forensic team assembled by the defendants was able to provide persuasive evidence that the debris in the suspected part was an artifact—that is, it had gotten into the engine part after the crash, perhaps during storage of the wreckage. The investigation was extensive and employed botanists, palynologists, chemists, and soil scientists. The jury was persuaded that the plaintiff's theory of the airplane part failure was not tenable.

An example of the application of forensic botany in a criminal case was in the Lindbergh kidnapping case, one of the earliest uses of plant evidence in a major case. At the time, 1932, this was one of the highest-profile cases in U.S. history. Charles Lindbergh was an American hero for having completed the first solo flight across the Atlantic Ocean in 1927. He had married Anne Morrow in 1929, and in 1930 they had had a son, Charles Jr. The family lived in Hopewell, New Jersey.

On the night of March 1 the baby was kidnapped. The kidnapper communicated with the family and demanded ransom. In consultation with police the family paid the ransom. An enormous effort was made to find the perpetrator. After several weeks the kidnapped baby was found dead. Eventually, a man named Bruno Hauptmann was charged.

The case was complicated, but there was considerable circumstantial evidence against Hauptmann. One item was a homemade ladder that had been used by the kidnapper to climb up to the second-floor nursery of the Lindbergh home and take the baby. The ladder was left behind at the scene. It was eventually turned over for examination to a wood expert named Arthur Koehler. He spent considerable time analyzing the features of the wood, both the natural ones and those that had been introduced by cutting and milling.

Once Hauptmann was arrested, police searched his house and seized a large amount of the ransom money secreted in his house. (The serial numbers of the bills had been recorded, so they were recognizable as the ransom money.) Police also seized boards from his attic. They thought boards that were missing from the attic might have been used to make the ladder. Koehler carefully compared the boards from the attic with those used to make the ladder and concluded that they came from the same source. While this example does not quite fit with the "transfer evidence" idea, it does show how knowledgeable experts can use wood comparisons to make strong associations. In this case the patterns in the wood told the story.

In most cases specialists identify the botanical evidence in terms of its species of origin and then see if any conclusion can be drawn. The sidebar "The Denise Johnson Case" in chapter 1 showed how this approach could be taken a step further, to use DNA methods to try to individualize the plant source. Plant DNA analysis is very uncommon at present, but it is likely that there will be more of it in the future.

Plant Materials in Foods: How They May Help Unravel Forensic Cases

There are two major ways that the plant materials in foods can help in forensic cases. The first is analysis of a decedent's stomach contents. Sometimes it is necessary to analyze stomach contents for the ingredients known to have been part of the person's last meal, and often these are materials of plant origin. Someone with botanical knowledge may be needed to help identify the plant ingredients of the stomach contents. Figuring out when a person had his or her last meal can be helpful in pinpointing the time of death. The components in the stomach contents may be consistent with a meal the decedent is known to have ingested. Using this information and information about how long it takes for the stomach to empty following a meal can help a pathologist estimate time of death.

The second way, as noted earlier, is to analyze fecal material for plant materials that are not digested. There are times when fecal material can be left at a crime scene or get onto clothing as a kind of "dried stain." In these cases specimens must be compared that are thought to be from the same original fecal specimen. If no constituent is found that is unique to either specimen, they could have come from the same source. This finding does not prove that the two samples did come from the same source, but it provides associative evidence. By the same token, if a unique constituent were present in one of the specimens, it would indicate that they did not have a common origin. These cases are comparatively unusual, but sometimes there is no other evidence that can help link an individual to a scene.

7

The Future

This chapter tries to look into the future of the changes in the nature of DNA profiling and how the ways it is used in forensic science might improve efficiency and increase the value of the analysis. Making the changes has potentially important implications for technology costs and for privacy concerns. The way DNA is used in criminal investigations could change if more analytical capability is brought to crime scenes. Enlarging the use of entomological and botanical evidence in investigations is also considered.

DIFFERENT DNA-TYPING METHODS: THE IMPLICATIONS OF TECHNOLOGY CHANGEOVERS

In previous chapters several DNA-typing and profiling methods were discussed. The most widely used techniques have relied on VNTR polymorphism, distinguishing people from one another on the basis of the number of tandem sequence repeats they have at several loci within DNA. The current techniques have speeded up the profiling process, but there are still backlogs in both casework and databasing.

There are other approaches to human identification, such as using single nucleotide polymorphisms (SNPs). Any change in technology that is intended for use in casework and in databases will take time to implement. Such a change would require that every specimen in every database be reprofiled using the new technology. Given the expense and effort of such an undertaking, the advantages of the new technology over the current one would have to be spectacular. Considering the current size of the databases and the effort involved in reprofiling all the specimens in them, it seems more likely that SNPs, like Y-chromosome markers and mtDNA, will serve as supplements to the core VNTR technology but not replace it, at least in the near future.

REDUCING BACKLOGS: DNA AUTOMATION AND ROBOTICS

As noted in chapter 5, DNA technology in the forensic science labs has not been able to keep up with casework and CODIS specimen demands. Even with quite a bit of federal assistance, laboratories have not been able to keep pace. Backlogs persist and even grow in some jurisdictions. Changes in laws that have broadened the range of offenses for which a person can be databased have also contributed to the backlog.

Some of the backlog problem has also been caused by decisions to go back through older cases, cases that were not originally processed in the laboratories, especially sexual assaults. The logic behind these initiatives is sound. By going back into old sexual assault evidence collection kits, pulling out semen evidence (if there is any), and profiling it, investigators will be able to make associations between related cases, and some of the cases may be solved because the profile will be found in a database. These efforts have yielded positive results, but they have contributed to the backlogs as well.

Given the volume of cases, DNA analysis must be done with high-specimen throughput (that is, with many specimens being analyzed simultaneously). Some laboratories have introduced robotics in an effort to reduce analysis time, and more will do so. Anything that can be done to reduce analysis time and effort will eventually be introduced. At the same time accuracy cannot be sacrificed to speed. Furthermore, the initial examination of the evidence and selection of the specimens for DNA analysis cannot be automated. Gains in speed and efficiency will come in the analytical stages, during extraction and profiling of the selected specimens.

High throughput is easier to achieve with database specimens, because every specimen is basically the same and can be processed identically. Some jurisdictions have contracted out the profiling of database specimens to independent laboratories in order to try to catch up. While catching up the backlog of older cases is a big job, they only have to be caught up once. Lab capacity will eventually adjust to being in synchrony with the number of cases being submitted, and forensic laboratories that conduct DNA profiling will eventually reach equilibrium between the work demanded and the work completed, but it may take a few more years.

ENLARGING DNA DATABASES: THE TRADE-OFFS BETWEEN LAW ENFORCEMENT AND CIVIL LIBERTIES

Some policy makers and law-enforcement officials are persuaded that databasing not just convicted offenders but arrestees and suspects would considerably increase the number of database matches and thus the solve rate of a number of types of cases. Experience in the United Kingdom, where suspects are databased, suggests that this expectation would be fulfilled. Many in the United States, however, oppose the practice as an infringement on citizens' civil liberties. Many see it as the start of a slide down a slippery slope to a place where the government holds too much information about its people, under the guise of public safety and law enforcement. There is certain to be much more of this debate.

The potential of DNA databases in promoting homeland security cannot be overlooked, either. A DNA profile is a unique identifier, but even people who might not object to the government having an identifier for a large number of its citizens worry about DNA serving as that identifier. There is considerable actual and potential information in DNA that, as noted throughout the book, is not exploited by the current technologies. Only a few jurisdictions have laws restricting what government laboratories can do with the DNA remaining in their possession once it has been profiled for the identifying data. Considerable information about a person is potentially obtainable from the DNA, information that goes well beyond identifying characteristics. A person's predilection for a disease or health condition, infection with HIV, and other such information could be obtained from DNA, now or in the near future. The current discussion is about whether there should there be laws restricting what government laboratories can do with DNA in their possession. The issue may become more pressing if more jurisdictions permit databasing of arrestees and suspects.

FIELD INSTRUMENTS: DNA TYPING AT THE SCENE?

Advances in miniaturization and microfluidics have enabled the creation of prototype devices no bigger than a wristwatch that can do DNA profiling. Miniaturization refers to the fabrication of instruments such as thermal cyclers, required for PCR, on a very much smaller scale. Microfluidics refers to the ability to make devices that can handle very small volumes of liquid—on a scale of nanoliters (billionths of a liter). In miniature devices that are hosts for biochemical reactions, such as PCR, the volumes of fluids involved are very small. Thus, microfluidics and instrument miniaturization go together to reduce the sizes of the instrument and the volumes of liquids involved. Together, these strategies can increase the speed of analysis.

DNA microarrays (chips), already used in biomedical research, might be fabricated for a variety of forensic purposes, and there is more to come. Such small, hand-held devices would almost certainly find use in the laboratory, but why not out in the field too? Why not put a DNA profiling instrument in the vehicle of every crime-scene unit? This concept, taking the laboratory and laboratory analyses to the scene, has the promise of improving efficiency of evidence processing.

Those who object to such technologies being used at scenes make the point that DNA profiling is complicated and that interpretation of the results by a scientist is necessary for the information to be properly used. Supporters simply point out that these devices would be available to provide investigative information and leads, not definitive DNA profiles for use in court. This problem could be avoided by having mobile laboratories. Instead of evidence being collected, packaged, labeled, and sent to a central laboratory for processing, what if a mobile lab were available to process the evidence onsite?

As the cost of these technologies comes down and availability increases, law-enforcement agencies will likely begin to embrace them. In theory, scene or mobile lab personnel could develop DNA profiles (even partial ones) from biological evidence and search databases for matches. They could search profiles from unsolved cases as well as profiles from convicted offenders. If a suspect database were available, that too could be searched for the scene profile. Although these things may sound futuristic, they are already being piloted in some European jurisdictions.

EXPANDED USE OF ENTOMOLOGY AND/OR BOTANICALS

For many years forensic science laboratories have requested more resources from their parent agencies and from the federal government. Until very recently politicians paid little attention to the issue. There has never been a very large constituency concerned with forensic science.

It has already been noted that there are significant backlog problems with DNA cases and databasing in many places, and it is fair to say that quite a bit of attention has been paid to providing resources for DNA, although backlogs persist. In the case of the specialties where the evidence does not come up very often, the situation is much worse. Within the scope of the material discussed in this book, entomology and botany are both underutilized. How much so? It is hard to say, because part of the reason the evidence does not come up very often might be because it is not looked for, not recognized, and thus never collected. If police investigators were massively trained in the recognition and collection of insect and botanical evidence, utilization would increase, but no one can really say by how much. It is hard to know how often these items might be important in a case.

Because entomological and botanical evidence is relatively uncommon in criminal investigations, few people have specialized in those subjects. After all, why would one encourage a young scientist to become a forensic entomologist or botanist if there are no full-time jobs in either specialty? But investigator training is important. The more that investigators become aware of the potential value of insect or botanical evidence, the more it is likely to be sought, recognized, collected, and submitted when appropriate. Simultaneously, it will be important for there to be specialists available to conduct the analyses in a timely way.

Perhaps ironically, the use of botanical evidence could grow because of DNA. DNA technology is expanding rapidly. In the future it will be applied to help individualize nonhuman specimens, such as hairs from household pets or plant materials. The more individuality that can be ascribed to an evidence item, the more useful it is in establishing positive associations, and the more likely it is to be utilized in criminal investigations.

GLOSSARY

acid phosphatase   an enzyme found in large quantities in human semen and often used as a preliminary test marker for the presence of semen

adsorption-elution   a method for the ABO typing of dried bloodstains

adsorption-inhibition   a method for the ABO typing and secretor status determination of body fluids

AFDIL (Armed Forces DNA Identification Laboratory)   the part of the Office of the Armed Forces Medical Examiner that performs DNA analysis on military human remains for identification

AFIP (Armed Forces Institute of Pathology)   the parent agency of the Office of the Armed Forces Medical Examiner that provides medical, medico-legal, and forensic services both to the military services and to outside agencies on request

AFIS (Automated Fingerprint Identification System)   a system that automatically matches unknown fingerprints against a database of known fingerprints

agglutination   the clumping or bridging together of red blood cells by antibodies specific for structures on the cell surfaces: The verb form is *agglutinate*.

allele   one of the members of a gene pair at a genetic locus

amino acid   a chemical that is a fundamental building block of proteins and enzymes

amplification   repetitive copying of a DNA segment using the polymerase chain reaction

amylase   an enzyme found in large quantities in saliva and used as a preliminary test marker for the presence of saliva

antibody   a protein produced by the immune system in response to the presence of an antigen. An antibody will specifically bind to the antigen that caused its production in order to disable the antigen.

antigen   a protein or other large biological molecule that can cause specific antibody formation in an animal

arc swing   a type of blood pattern caused by swinging a bloody object; also known as cast off. The pattern is medium velocity, but the droplets will have struck the surface at a series of angles as the object is swung through the air and blood droplets fly from it.

arterial spurt   a type of blood pattern caused by a severed artery spurting blood onto a surface, following each of the contractions of the heart

autoradiography   the process of exposing X-ray film by radioactivity. This method was formerly used to detect DNA on Southern blots in the RFLP method of DNA typing.

biopolymer   any large polymer molecule (molecule composed of smaller repeating units) that is made by a living organism. Proteins, nucleic acids, and carbohydrates are examples of biopolymers.

blood type   a genetically determined characteristic of human blood, defined by specific antigen structures on the surface of the red blood cell. The four major human blood types are A, B, AB, and O.

blunt-force injury   an injury caused by a blunt object that strikes, falls on, or crashes into a person

capillary electrophoresis (CE)   electrophoresis in a very small capillary tube, used in forensic science to separate amplified DNA fragments for the VNTR method of DNA typing

carrion   the flesh of a dead animal (including a dead human being)

cast off   *See* ARC SWING

catalyst   a chemical that speeds up a chemical reaction. Enzymes are protein catalysts.

CE   *See* CAPILLARY ELECTROPHORESIS

chain extension   the final step in the polymerase chain reaction, in which the action of the Taq polymerase completes the synthesis of primed DNA segments

chain of custody   a business record of the location and custodian of an evidence item at every point from its initial seizure to its introduction in the courtroom. The chain of custody establishes that the evidence is original and intact.

chromatography   literally, "writing with color"; a technique for separating chemical compounds based on the interactions of these compounds as they move in a mobile phase (a gas or a liquid) that is associated with a stationary phase (a polymer used to pack the chromatography column). Gas chromatography, paper chromatography, thin-layer chromatography, and liquid chromatography are examples.

chromosome   one of the physical structures in the nucleus of a cell that carries the DNA. In humans there are 23 pairs of chromosomes, including the sex chromosomes (X and Y).

CILHI   *See* JPAC

class   a defined group of items that are similar to one another because similar processes were used to make them

class characteristics   those features that all members of a class share

cocoon   a common name for puparium, the container that holds an insect during the pupa stage of its life cycle

CODIS (Combined DNA Indexing System)   the DNA databases containing profiles from convicted offenders and unsolved cases, coordinated by the FBI and used and maintained by many law-enforcement agencies by way of their forensic science laboratories

common origin   a situation in which two or more items were originally part of a single item (or person). The process of determining that items are from a common origin is known as individualization.

contact transfer   a blood pattern that is created when an object comes into contact with a bloody surface, leaving a pattern of itself in the bloodstain

creatinine   a chemical excreted in measurable quantities in human urine. Its presence in an unknown specimen indicates that the specimen might be urine

criminalistics   the evaluation of physical evidence in legal matters; primarily the evaluation of patterns, materials, forensic biology, and forensic chemistry

crossing over   a phenomenon that occurs during meiosis, in which sister chromatids (duplicated chromosomes) physically exchange portions of their structures when they are paired up. Crossing over increases the genetic diversity of the resulting sperm or egg cells

denaturation   separation of the strands of double-stranded DNA, also called melting. Strand separation is necessary to replicate DNA strands.

deoxyribonucleic acid   *See* DNA

differential extraction   the isolation of epithelial cell DNA and sperm cell DNA from a mixture of the sperm and epithelial cells. Differential extraction allows a forensic biologist to separately type male and female DNA

disputed parentage   a situation in which it is uncertain whether a particular person is the parent of a particular child. Usually disputed parentage cases involve disputed paternity (fatherhood is in question).

DNA (deoxyribonucleic acid)   the genetic material of living things. DNA is a large polymer of nucleotides arranged as a double-stranded helix structure.

DNA database   a computerized collection of the DNA profiles of either convicted offenders or unknown persons (probable perpetrators) in unsolved cases. A database could contain the profiles of missing persons or of their relatives.

DNA polymerase   an enzyme that catalyzes DNA replication

DNA profile   a combination of DNA types at several loci. When the probability of chance duplication of a profile greatly exceeds the number of persons in the population, a DNA profile can essentially be regarded as unique.

DNA typing   the process of determining the fragment sizes of DNA that has been cut or amplified from a specific locus, providing the genetic type at that locus

electrophoresis   a procedure that uses an electric field in a gel or other medium to separate charged macromolecules (such as proteins or nucleic acids) based on their net charge

entomotoxicology   the determination of what drugs or toxins are present in the larvae of carrion-feeding insects in order to find out what drugs or toxins were present in the dead body on which they were found

enzyme   a protein that catalyzes a specific reaction in the cell

epithelial cells   flat, nucleated cells that line body cavities and ducts and also make up the skin

exemplar   a specimen of known origin, used for comparison with specimens whose origin is not known

extraction   in DNA testing, the isolation of DNA from a biological specimen

forensic anthropology the study of the structure and evolution of the human skeleton as it relates to identifying persons from skeletal remains

forensic biology generally, the forensic examination of blood, body fluids, or other biological evidence for purposes of individualization using genetic typing. The term is also used to mean the evaluation, identification, and species testing of biological evidence leading up to DNA typing.

forensic botany the analysis of plant and plant part evidence to help answer legal questions

forensic entomology the analysis of insect evidence to help answer legal questions

gene in classical genetics, the unit of inherited material that determines some characteristic in an organism. It corresponds to a segment of DNA, not necessarily contiguous on the chromosome, that is responsible for production of a particular protein or polypeptide chain. It can be a continuous DNA segment containing a series of head-to-tail repeat sequences.

genetic code the triplet sequence of bases in messenger RNA (mRNA; the intermediary nucleic acid that translates the DNA sequence into an amino acid sequence in protein) that specifies each amino acid in protein. There are 64 "words," or triplets, in the genetic code.

genome the total DNA in the nucleus of an organism

hemoglobin the primary oxygen-transporting protein of animal blood, found in red blood cells

heterozygous having different genes (alleles) on the paternal and maternal chromosomes at a particular locus in DNA. The noun form is *heterozygote*.

high-velocity blood pattern a pattern of blood caused by an extreme force (such as a bullet impact or explosion) applied to pooled blood, which projects the blood through the air and breaks it into numerous and very small (aerosol spray–size) droplets

histocompatibility the compatibility of tissue antigens between persons, in the context of tissue and organ transplantation

homozygous having identical genes (alleles) on the paternal and maternal chromosomes at a particular locus in DNA. The noun form is *homozygote*.

hybridization   one-to-one base pairing of a single-stranded DNA with another, complementary strand, usually a primer or probe

hydrolysis   a decomposition reaction in which the addition of the elements of water (H and OH) across a chemical bond breaks the bond

identification   in criminalistics, assigning an item to a particular class; for example, a stain might be identified as blood, or a fiber, as nylon. With reference to human remains, the word means individualization (as in, "the body was identified as that of John Doe").

imago   an insect in the adult stage of its life cycle

independent assortment   the principle of inheritance known as Mendel's second law, which states that the separation of one chromosome pair into daughter cells during meiosis is not influenced by the assortment of any other chromosome pair

individual characteristics   those features of a person, item, or object that can render it unique among members of its class

individualization   the process of establishing that an item or person is unique among the members of its class

insect life cycle   the stages of an insect's entire life, from egg to larva to pupa to adult (imago). All insects have a life cycle that goes through these stages.

isoelectric focusing   a technique similar to electrophoresis, but based on a different principle, that is used to separate proteins

isoenzyme   any of multiple molecular forms of the same enzyme. Before DNA typing existed forensic scientists used isoenzymes in blood and body fluids to help individualize biological evidence.

JPAC (Joint POW/MIA Accounting Command)   the forensic anthropology laboratory of the U.S. Armed Forces, whose main mission is to recover and identify the remains of U.S. service members killed abroad; formerly called Central Identification Laboratory Hawaii (CILHI)

known   in forensic science, a specimen whose origin is certain; also called an exemplar

larva   a stage in the life cycle of an insect, equivalent to maggot

locus (*plural*, **loci**)   a particular region of DNA, occupied by a gene responsible for a particular product or function, or VNTR

low-velocity blood pattern   a pattern of blood caused by droplets falling due to the force of gravity alone

maggot   a common name for larva

medium-velocity blood pattern   a pattern of blood that occurs when medium force is applied to pooled blood, projecting droplets through the air. Medium-velocity patterns have more and smaller stains than low-velocity patterns.

meiosis   reduction cell division; the process by which a cell replicates its chromosomes, then divides twice to make germ cells (sperm or egg) that contain only half the original chromosome number

microsatellite   *See* SHORT TANDEM REPEAT

mitochondrial DNA (mtDNA)   the DNA of a cell's mitochondrion

mitochondrion (*plural,* **mitochondria)**   a membrane-bounded structure within the cell that contains the biochemical machinery to process energy for cell activities. A cell has many mitochondria, and mitochondria have their own DNA.

mitosis   cell division. Mitosis produces two daughter cells that are identical to the parent cell.

mitotype   the sequence of bases at the variable regions in mitochondrial DNA. A mitotype represents the combination of individual differences in mtDNA.

molecular genetics   knowledge of inheritance mechanisms at the molecular level, involving DNA, RNA, and proteins

mtDNA   *See* MITOCHONDRIAL DNA

multiplex PCR   amplification, using the polymerase chain reaction, of more than one locus at a time in the same tube

mutation   a random change in a base in DNA that permanently changes the sequence. Mutation is ultimately responsible for the individual differences in DNA.

nucleic acid   a term referring to either DNA or RNA

nucleotide   a molecule consisting of a purine or pyrimidine base (A, T, C, or G), phosphoric acid, and ribose sugar. Nucleotides are the building blocks of DNA and RNA.

nucleus   the membrane-bounded structure within the cell that contains the chromosomes, which in turn contain all the nuclear DNA

palynology   the study of plant pollens

parentage testing   genetic testing to include or exclude paternity or maternity

PCR   *See* POLYMERASE CHAIN REACTION

plasma   the liquid, noncellular portion of blood, containing the clotting proteins

polymer   large molecule composed of simpler repeating-unit molecules bonded together in a chain

polymerase chain reaction (PCR)   replication of a small segment of DNA into a large number of copies using a thermostable DNA polymerase and sequence-specific primers. The three steps are strand separation, primer annealing, and chain extension.

polymorphism   genetic variation within the same species. Polymorphism is the basis for using genetic typing to individualize biological evidence.

primer   a single-stranded segment of DNA that defines one end of a larger segment of DNA to be copied by the polymerase chain reaction

primer annealing   the process by which a primer binds its complementary sequence in a segment of DNA

probe   a singe-stranded segment of DNA designed to bind to a specific place (its complementary sequence) within DNA in order to detect that portion of DNA

protein   one of the several important classes of biopolymers. Proteins consist of amino acids and can be structural entities or enzymes in the cell.

pupa   a stage in the life cycle of an insect, contained in a cocoon, or puparium

questioned   in forensic science, a specimen of unknown origin. A questioned specimen is compared with a known to include or exclude common origin.

real-time PCR (RT-PRCR)   a method for determining the quantity of human DNA in a specimen using the polymerase chain reaction among other applications. In other contexts, the abbreviation *RT-PCR* is sometimes used to refer to reverse transcriptase PCR.

recombination   the redistribution of genes in daughter cells following meiosis as a result of crossing over

reconstruction in forensic science, the use of physical evidence and its analysis to reconstruct past events

red blood cell a blood cell that contains hemoglobin. Mature red blood cells lack a nucleus and cannot reproduce by cell division. They are continuously replaced by the body.

restriction endonuclease an enzyme that hydrolyzes double-stranded DNA at a specific sequence of bases, cutting it into two pieces. It is used in the RFLP method of DNA typing.

restriction fragment length polymorphism (RFLP) the first forensic DNA-typing technology, this procedure treats DNA with a restriction enzyme, separates the resulting DNA fragments using electrophoresis, fixes them in place using Southern blotting, and then estimates the fragments' sizes (that are proportional to VNTR numbers) at certain loci.

RFLP *See* RESTRICTION FRAGMENT LENGTH POLYMORPHISM

ribonucleic acid *See* RNA

RNA (ribonucleic acid) a single-stranded polymer of nucleotides similar in composition to DNA, except that the nucleotide uracil (U) is found instead of the base thymine (T)

RT-PCR *See* REAL-TIME PCR

secretor an individual who has the genetic makeup to synthesize ABO blood group substances in his or her body fluids. The term is misleading because the blood group substances are not actually "secreted" from anywhere, but it is entrenched in the technical language of the field.

segregation the principle of inheritance known as Mendel's first law, which states that the genes in a pair of chromosomes are discrete and separate cleanly into separate germ cells during meiosis

semen the male reproductive fluid, containing the spermatozoa

seminal fluid the liquid portion of semen

sequencing the process of determining the order of the units in a biological polymer, such as the nucleotides in mitochondrial DNA or in a segment of DNA or RNA, or the amino acids in a protein

serum the liquid (noncellular) portion of blood without the clotting proteins. When whole blood clots, the liquid component that remains is serum.

sex chromosomes the pair of chromosomes known as X and Y that together determine whether an animal is female (XX) or male (XY). Strictly speaking, X and Y are different, and XY is not a true pair.

short tandem repeat (STR) a two-, three-, four-, or five-base sequence that is repeated head to tail at a locus in DNA; also called a microsatellite. Four- and five-base pair repeats are used for forensic identification.

single nucleotide polymorphism (SNP) a genetic difference between persons that consists of a single base difference at a particular location in DNA (sometimes SNP is pronounced as "snip")

SNP *See* SINGLE NUCLEOTIDE POLYMORPHISM

Southern blotting a technique for transferring of DNA fragments from a gel to a nitrocellulose or nylon membrane. The fragments retain the same orientation on the membrane as on the gel and are tightly bound, so they can be manipulated for further testing.

spermatozoan (*plural*, spermatozoa) the male reproductive cell

STR *See* SHORT TANDEM REPEAT

succession in forensic entomology, a natural process in which a series of insect species invade a dead body following a certain predictable sequence, as one species alters the body such that it is then attractive to the next species

swipe pattern a type of blood pattern caused by the movement of certain objects with multiple bristles or hairs. When such an object moves across an existing pool of wet blood, or when the object is itself wet with blood and moves across a surface, it leaves a swipe pattern.

tandem repeat a head-to-tail repeat of a base sequence in DNA. A four-base tandem repeat could be, for example, . . . GTCCGTCC-GTCCGTCCGTCC . . . , where GTCC is the repeating unit.

transcription synthesis of a complementary strand of RNA from a strand of DNA

translation synthesis of a protein in which the base sequence in the messenger RNA (mRNA) specifies the order of amino acids in the protein

unknown in forensic science, a specimen of uncertain origin, requiring identification (classification) and/or comparison with a known standard to try to individualize it; also called questioned

urea   a chemical excreted in measurable quantities in human urine. Its presence indicates that an unknown specimen might contain urine.

variable number of tandem repeats (VNTR)   the type of polymorphism in DNA that forensic scientists use for human identification. Individuals differ on the basis of the number of repeats they have at certain specific DNA loci.

vasectomy   a surgical procedure that disconnects the tubes carrying a male's sperm to the seminal vesicles. The result is that the male's semen has no sperm, and he is sterile.

VNTR   *See* VARIABLE NUMBER OF TANDEM REPEATS

wipe pattern   a type of blood pattern caused by the movement of some object across an existing pool of wet blood or the movement across a surface of an object that is itself wet with blood

FURTHER READING

Anslinger, K., G. Weichhold, W. Keil, B. Bayer, and W. Eisenmenger. "Identification of the skeletal remains of Martin Bormann by mtDNA analysis." *International Journal of Legal Medicine* 114 (2001): 194–196. Describes how forensic scientists identified a buried body as that of Bormann.

Arlington National Cemetery Web site. "'Unknown Soldier' Is Michael Joseph Blassie." Available online. URL: http://www.arlington cemetery.net/unk-vn43.htm. Accessed August 29, 2007. Describes how the Armed Forces DNA Identification Lab used mitochondrial DNA typing to identify the "unknown soldier" from the Vietnam War.

Bock, Jane H., and David O. Norris. "Forensic botany: An under-utilized resource." *Journal of Forensic Sciences* 42 (1997): 364–367. Describes some of the potential uses of botanical evidence in forensic casework.

Brenner, Charles H. "World Trade Center Disaster Identification Diary." Available online. URL: http://dna-view.com/wtcdiary.htm. Accessed August 29, 2007. Describes the efforts to identify victims of the September 11, 2001, attack, as recorded by forensic mathematician Charles Brenner. According to Brenner, about 1,500 people had been identified as of June 24, 2003, something like one-third of them by DNA methods.

Brkic, H., D. Strinovic, M. Kubat, and V. Petrovecki. "Odontological identification of human remains from mass graves in Croatia." *International Journal of Legal Medicine* 114 (2000): 19–22. Describes how forensic dentists make identifications of human remains from mass graves—in this case, in Croatia, formerly part of Yugoslavia.

Catts, E. Paul, and Neal H. Haskell. *Entomology and Death: A Procedural Guide*. Clemson, S.C.: Joyce's Print Shop, 1990. A detailed field guide for investigators.

Cranshaw, W. S., and F. B. Peairs. "Flies in the Home." Colorado State University Cooperative Extension. Available online. URL: http://www.ext.colostate.edu/pubs/insect/05502.html. Accessed September 3, 2007. An illustrated discussion and quick facts about some common flies and their life cycles.

Fisher, D. L., M. M. Holland, L. Mitchell, et al. "Extraction, evaluation, and amplification of DNA from decalcified and undecalcified United States Civil War bone." *Journal of Forensic Sciences* 38 (1993): 60–68. A detailed paper describing how scientists isolated DNA from human bones more than 100 years old and obtained DNA-typing information from the specimens.

Goff, M. L. *A Fly for the Prosecution: How Insect Evidence Helps Solve Crimes.* Cambridge, Mass.: Harvard University Press, 2000. An introduction to forensic entomology that also reports of cases in which Goff was the expert.

Graham, Alan. "Forensic palynology and the Ruidoso, New Mexico plane crash—The pollen evidence II." *Journal of Forensic Sciences* 42 (1997): 391–393. Illustrates how pollen evidence was used in the reconstruction of a small plane crash.

Graham, Shirley A. "Anatomy of the Lindbergh kidnapping." *Journal of Forensic Sciences* 42 (1997): 368–377. Summarizes the primary forensic evidence in the Lindbergh kidnapping case and how it implicated Bruno Hauptmann.

Gross, Hans. *Criminal Investigation.* London: Sweet and Maxwell, 1924. One of the earliest, classic books to develop the principles of criminalistics.

Helmer, R. P. "Identification of the cadaver remains of Josef Mengele." *Journal of Forensic Sciences* 32 (1987): 1,622–1,644. Describes how forensic scientists identified a buried body as that of the Nazi doctor Josef Mengele.

Hickman, Matthew J., and Joseph L. Peterson. *50 Largest Crime Labs, 2002.* Washington, D.C.: U.S. Department of Justice, Office of Justice Programs, Bureau of Justice Statistics, 2004.

Holland, M. M., D. L. Fisher, L. G. Mitchell, et al. "Mitochondrial DNA sequence analysis of human skeletal remains: identification of remains from the Vietnam War." *Journal of Forensic Sciences* 38 (1993): 542–553. Describes the AFIP laboratory's methods and techniques in using mtDNA typing to identify unknown remains from the Vietnam theater of war.

Kakesako, Gregg K. "Hickam Lab IDs Unknown Soldier." Starbulletin. com. Available online. URL: http://starbulletin.com/2003/05/22/ news/story11.html. Accessed August 29, 2007. Describes how X-ray and odontological techniques were used by CILHI to identify the first "unknown soldier" from the Korean War.

Lewis, Walter H. "Pollen composition in a crashed plane's engine." *Journal of Forensic Sciences* 42 (1997): 387–390. Describes the utility of pollen analysis in reconstructing a small plane crash.

National Institute of Justice. "The Future of Forensic DNA Testing: Predictions of the Research and Development Working Group, NCJ–183697." November 2000. The report discusses past and present techniques in forensic DNA analysis, the most likely technical advances in the forthcoming decade, and assesses the impact of these advances on forensic DNA analysis.

———. "National Forensic DNA Study Report: Final Report to the National Institute of Justice on Grant 2002-LT-BX-K 003." December 2003. A research report submitted to the U.S. Department of Justice on the need for law enforcement agencies to review old cases for potential biological evidence that should be sent to a crime laboratory for testing.

———. "Report to the Attorney General on Delays in Forensic DNA Analysis, NCJ-199425." March 2003. This report presents the results of a task force, convened by the NIJ at the request of Attorney General John Ashcroft, to assess existing DNA analysis delays and develop recommendations for eliminating those delays.

Norris, David O., and Jane H. Bock. "Use of fecal material to associate a suspect with a crime scene: Report of two cases." *Journal of Forensic Sciences* 45 (2000): 184–187. Describes how fecal material from a scene was used to associate a suspect to the crime; an example of using botanical evidence.

Peterson, Joseph L., and Matthew J. Hickman. *Census of Publicly Funded Forensic Crime Laboratories, 2002.* Washington, D.C.: U.S. Department of Justice, Office of Justice Programs, Bureau of Justice Statistics, 2005.

Primorac, Dragan, et al. "Identification of war victims from mass graves in Croatia, Bosnia, and Herzegovina by use of standard forensic methods and DNA typing." *Journal of Forensic Sciences* 41 (1996): 891–894. Discusses the identification of human remains in mass graves from the period when the former Yugoslavia was collapsing and independent countries were developing. Traditional methods and DNA typing were both employed.

Rainio, Juha, et al. "Forensic osteological investigations in Kosovo." *Forensic Science International* 121 (2001): 166–173. Describes the analysis of human skeletal remains in Kosovo (formerly part of Yugoslavia) to identify the victims of the war there.

Thornton, John I. "Criminalistics: Past, present, and future." *Lex et Scientia* 11 (1975): 1–44. A comprehensive paper on understanding criminalistics and its conceptual basis.

———. "The general assumptions and rationale of forensic science." In *Modern Scientific Evidence,* edited by David L. Faigman, David H. Kaye, Michael J. Saks, and Joseph Sanders. St. Paul, Minn.: West Publishing, 1997. An updated comprehensive paper on understanding the theory and basis of forensic sciences and forensic practice.

Wambaugh, Joseph. *The Blooding.* New York: Bantam, 1989. Describes the Narborough murders in the United Kingdom and the use of forensic DNA typing by Alec Jeffreys for the first time in a criminal case.

Weedn, V. W. "Postmortem identifications of remains." *Clinical and Laboratory Medicine* 18 (1998): 115–137. Discusses the methods for identifying human remains and the relative value and utility of each.

Web Sites

DNA from the Beginning. Available online. URL: http://www.dnaftb.org/dnaftb/. Accessed July 28, 2004. A Web site set up by Cold Spring Harbor Laboratory, covering DNA from classical genetics to modern concepts and incorporating animated graphics. This site is a good place to do a basic genetics and molecular genetics tutorial online.

Electronic Scholarly Publishing. Available online. URL: http://www.esp.
org/. Accessed August 29, 2007. Contains full text of many of the
classic papers in human genetics.

President's DNA Initiative. Available online. URL: http://www.dna.
gov/info/. Accessed July 13, 2007. The official Web site of the U.S.
president's program to assure accuracy and fairness in the criminal
justice system through the use of DNA technology. This site provides
detailed information on the initiative, its grant funding, and some of
the results that have been obtained thus far.

INDEX

Italic page numbers indicate illustrations

A

A (adenine) 55
ABI COfiler kit 110, *113*
ABI Profiler kit 110, *112*
ABO blood typing 21–32, 38, 39
absorption-elution 24–25
acid phosphatase 80–81
Adams, Holly Marie 126
adenine (A) 55
Adler, Oskar and Rudolf 18
adsorption-inhibition 27
affiliation 125–127
AFIP (Armed Forces Institute of Pathology) 129
AFIS (Automated Fingerprint Identification System) 128
African Americans 29, 64
agarose gel 70
agglutination 23, 27
airplane crashes 143–144
algae 143
allele 53
amino acid 57, 59
amplification 106–107
amylase 21, 85–86
animal blood 87
antibody 21, 23–27, 34, 88
anticodon 57
antigen 23–27
antiserum 88
Arbois, Bergert d' 17

arc swing 93
Armed Forces DNA Identification Laboratory (AFDIL) 129, 130
Armed Forces Institute of Pathology (AFIP) 129
arterial spurt 93
Ashcroft, John 120
autoradiogram 72, 105–106
Avery, Oswald T. 43, 44

B

backlogs
    in DNA profiling cases/databases 118, 120–121, 147–148
    future issues 150
    and species testing 88–89
    and STR typing 109
bacteria 98
base pairs 62–63, 67–68
base temperature 133
Beadle, George 42
beetles 136, 137, 141
best evidence 78–79, 123, 125
biopolymer 32
BJS (Bureau of Justice Statistics) 121
Blassie, Michael 130
blood
    DNA typing of 8–9
    early forensic research 18–19
    and forensic entomology 11–12
    preliminary testing 75–94
    and species testing 87–89
    typing of. *See* ABO blood typing
blood-feeding insects 11–12

blood-spatter patterns xv, xvi, 9–10,
    89–94, *90, 92*
bloodstains 18, 38–39
blood typing. *See* ABO blood typing
blowflies 136, 140
blunt-force injury 91–93
body fluids. *See* physiological fluids
Bogan, Mark 14
botany. *See* forensic botany
bread mold 42–43
Bridges, Calvin 42
Buckland, Rodney 48
Bureau of Justice Statistics (BJS) 121

C

C (cytosine) 55
capillary electrophoresis (CE) 72–73,
    109–110
carrion insect 10–11, 133
cast off. *See* arc swing
catalyst 34
catalytic tests 79–80
caterpillar 138–139
Caucasians 29, 39, 65
CE. *See* capillary electrophoresis
Central Identification Laboratory Hawaii
    (CILHI) 129, 130
Cetus Corporation 50, 107
chain extension 68
chain of custody 76
chemiluminescence 80
China, ancient 16
chloroform 96
chromatography 32
chromosome 42, 51, 52, 60, 61
CILHI. *See* Central Identification
    Laboratory Hawaii
civil liberties 116, 148–149
class characteristics 128
cocoon 11, 133
CODIS (Combined DNA Indexing Sys-
    tem) 116–118, 120, 122, 147
codon 57, 58

cold hit 117
Collins, Francis 45
color test 18
Combined DNA Indexing System. *See*
    CODIS
complementary sequence 57, 59
confirmatory tests 79
Congress, U.S. 115, 116
contact transfer 93–94
contamination 76, 114
creatinine 21, 86
Crick, Francis 43, 55
criminalistics 3–8
crossing over *54, 55*
Crowell-Webb, Cathleen 28
cytosine (C) 55

D

database 7–8, 146, 147. *See also* DNA
    profile databases
Deen, J. Izaak van 18
degradation
    and DNA quantitation 97–98
    and gel methods of DNA manipu-
        lation 70
    and mtDNA typing 112
    and PCR 107
    and RLFP 106
    and RT-PCR 99
    and Y-chromosome markers 114–115
degree-days 133–136
denaturation 68
dental records 127, 128
deoxyribonucleic acid (DNA). *See* DNA
Dermestes lardarius 141
differential extraction 114–115
digest (DNA extraction) 96
disputed parentage. *See* parentage testing
DNA (deoxyribonucleic acid)
    analysis/manipulation of 65–73
    and forensic botany 150
    gel methods for visualizing 70–71
    as genetic material 44, 51–74

mitochondrial. *See* mitochondrial
  DNA
and protein synthesis 43, 57, *59*
replication 66–68, *67*
separation, labeling, and detection of
  segments 71–73
structural variation in different
  people 58, 60
structure/function of 55–61, *56*
variation of interest to forensic
  scientists 60–61
DNA chip 131, 149
DNA fingerprints 46–47
DNA microarray 131, 149
DNA polymerase 50, 58
DNA probe 72, *73*, 101
DNA profile databases xvii, 115–118,
  120–121, 147–149
DNA quantitation 97–99, *99*
DNA sequencing 45
DNA typing xvii, 95–131
  applications 8–9, 118–119, 122–130
  backlogs in cases/databases 120–
    121, 147–148
  databases. *See* DNA profile databases
  DNA extraction 96–97
  DNA preparation 95–99
  DNA quantitation 97–99, *99*
  dot-blot technology 107–108, *108*
  future issues 146–150
  history of 45–50
  human remains identification 119,
    127–130
  interpretation of results 123, 125
  known/unknown specimens 7
  mtDNA for 111–114, *112, 113,*
    122–123, 127, 130
  and Narborough murders 48–49
  parentage/affiliation cases 9, 119,
    125–127
  PCR for 101–102, 106–107
  replacement of previous typing
    methods by 37

for resolving criminal cases 119,
  122–123
RFLP for 48, 65, 100, 102–106, *104,*
  105
SNP for 131, 147
STR for 108–111
Y-chromosome markers for 114–115
documentation of evidence 5, 75–76
dot-blot DNA typing 107–108, *108*
Dotson, Gary 28, 122
double helix 55, *56*
dried blood 26
Drosophila melanogaster 42
drowning victims 143
drug evidence 140

E
electrophoresis 32–34, *33*, 70, 103
entomology xv. *See also* forensic
  entomology
*Entomology and Death: A Procedural
  Guide* (Lord) 137
entomotoxicology 11, 137
enzyme 21, 35–36
Ephedra nevandensis pollen 142
epithelial cells 21, 114
ethyl alcohol 96
European criminal justice system 3–4
evidence
  collection of 82–84
  preparation of DNA from 95–99
  principles of handling 75–77
  searching/evaluation 77–79
examining magistrate 4
exclusion
  ABO typing 30–32
  bloodstains 38–39
  DNA typing 122, 123
  parentage testing 126
  specimen comparison 7
exemplar 7
exoneration 122, 123
exonuclease 101–102

explosions, high-velocity blood pattern
from 91
extraction 95–97

F
false positive 79
FBI (Federal Bureau of Investigation) 17
fecal matter 13, 145
fecal samples 17
Federal Bureau of Investigation (FBI) 17
fingerprints 127, 128
flies 10, 11, 133, *134*, 136, 137
fluids, body. *See* physiological fluids
fluorescent tag 101, 102
foods, plant materials in 12–13, 145
forensic anthropology 128
forensic biology, in preliminary
examinations 77
forensic botany 12–13, 140–145
early history 17
future possibilities for 150
minor role of 3, 15
plant materials in foods 145
"trace and transfer" evidence 141–145
forensic DNA analysis. *See* DNA typing
forensic entomology xvii, 3, 10–12, 15, 17,
132–141, 150
forensic file 116–117, 122
forensic mtDNA typing 62
forensic science (definition) 1
forensic toxicology 11, 18, 137
fruit fly 42
future issues 146–150

G
G (guanine) 55
gels 33, 70–71, 97–98, 103, 105
gene 41, 52
genetic code 57
genetics xvi, 37, 39–45, 51–74
genome 45, 51
globe mallow pollen 142
Greenberg, Bernard 17

Gross, Hans 4
guanine (G) 55
gunshot wounds 91

H
hair 62, 113
Hall, D. G. 17
haplotype 115
haptoglobin (HP) 35
Hardy, Godfrey Harold 63
Hardy-Weinberg equilibrium 63–64
Hauptmann, Bruno 144
Helentjaris, Timothy 14
hemoglobin 79–80
hemolytic anemia 24
heterozygous allele 53, 54, 102, 106
high-velocity blood pattern 91
histocompatibility locus region 37
history, of forensic biology 16–50
ABO blood typing 21–32
chromatography 32
DNA and protein synthesis 43–44
DNA typing 45–50
early history 16–21
electrophoresis 33–34
genetics 37, 40–44
Human Genome Project 45
isoenzymes 35–39
Alec Jeffreys's work 46–47
Gregor Mendel's inheritance studies
40–42
molecular genetics 42–43
PCR typing 49–50
serum protein polymorphisms 34–35
HLA (human leukocyte antigen) 36
Holley, Robert 43
homeland security 148
homozygous allele 53, 54
Hoover, J. Edgar 17
HP (haptoglobin) 35
human genome 51
Human Genome Project 45, 60
human leukocyte antigen (HLA) 36

human remains, identification of 9, 119, 127–130
human-specific DNA profiling 89
hybridization 72
hydrolysis 65
hypervariable regions 62, 63

I

identification (classification) 79–81, 85–87
imago 11
immunology 21, 34, 87–88
inclusion 28–29, 38–39, 123
independent assortment 55
individualization 79
inheritance xvi, 40–42, 51–55, 62–63
insect life cycle xvii, 11, 133–137, *134*
insect succession 136
instar 133
interpretation of DNA test results 123
interspersed sequences 60
isoelectric focusing 34
isoenzyme 35–39
isoleucine 58

J

Jeffreys, Sir Alec xvi, 46–47, 100
John, Adam 138
Johnson, Denise 14
Joint POW/MIA Accounting Command (JPAC) Central Identification Laboratory 129
junk DNA 45–47

K

Khorana, H. G. 43
Kind, Stuart 24
known (term) 7
Koehler, Arthur 144–145

L

Landsteiner, Karl xv–xvi, 21–23, *22*
larva 11, 133
Lattes, Leone 24, *25*, 26

Lattes test 26
LDIS (Local DNA Indexing System) 117
Lederberg, Joshua 43
Li, Li 126
Lilledahl, Ronald 130
Lindbergh, Charles 144
Lindbergh kidnapping case 144–145
linkage equilibrium 64
Local DNA Indexing System (LDIS) 117
locus/loci
    DNA profile databases 117–118
    DNA profiling 8–9
    dot-blot DNA typing 107–108
    inheritance 52–55
    linkage equilibrium 64
    parentage testing 126–127
    RLFP typing 102, 106
    STR typing 110, 111
Lord, Wayne 137, 139
low-velocity blood pattern 91
luminol 80
lymphocytes 37

M

MacLeod, Colin M. 43, 44
maggot 11, 12, 133, 137, 139. *See also* larva
marijuana 140
maternal inheritance 111, 112
McCarty, Maclyn 43, 44
medium-velocity blood pattern 91
meiosis 52, *53*, 55
membrane, for Southern blotting 71
Mendel, Gregor *40*, 40–42, 52
Mendel's laws 42, 52, 55
messenger RNA (mRNA) 57, 59
microfluidics 149
microsatellites 109
military personnel 9, 129, 130
Miller, Raymon and Richard 126
miniaturization 149
miniconcentrator 96
minigel 97–98
mitochondrial DNA (mtDNA)

as alternative to nuclear DNA typing 122–123
DNA typing by 111–114
and genetics 61–63
for identifying human remains 127, 130
mitosis 52, *53*
mitotype 111, 113–114, 123
mobile DNA laboratories 149–150
molecular genetics 42–43
Morgan, Thomas Hunt 42
Mormon tea pollen 142
mRNA. *See* messenger RNA
mtDNA. *See* mitochondrial DNA
Muller, H. J. 42
Mullis, Kary 49–50, 66
multiplex PCR 109
mutation 46, 60, 62

N
Narborough, England murders 47–49
National DNA Indexing System (NDIS) 117
National Institute of Justice (NIJ) 120, 121
NDIS (National DNA Indexing System) 117
Neurospora crassa 42
NIJ (National Institute of Justice) 120, 121
Nirenberg, Marshall 43
nonfunctional DNA. *See* junk DNA
nonsecretor 27–29
nuclear DNA profiling 127
nucleated cell 96
nucleic acid 32
nucleotide 57

O
Orfila, Mathieu-Joseph-Bonaventure xv, 18, *19*
Ouchterlony, Örjan 88
Ouchterlony dish 88

P
packaging 76
paloverde tree 14
palynology 142
parentage testing 9, 119, 125–127
Patterson, Ponte 138–139
PCR. *See* polymerase chain reaction
peptide bond 59
PerkinElmer 107
PGM 37
phenol 96
physiological fluids. *See also specific fluids, e.g.: semen*
    ABO typing 27–32
    DNA typing 8–9
    early forensic research 19–21
    preliminary testing 75–94
pine pollen 142
Pitchfork, Colin 49
plants. *See* forensic botany
plasma 23
PM (Polymarker) 108
PMI. *See* postmortem interval
pneumococcus 44
pollen grains 142, *143*
polymer 32, 57
polymerase chain reaction (PCR) 49–50, 65–70, *69,* 101–102, 106–107. *See also* real-time PCR
polymorphism
    and blood typing 21
    in DNA 58, 60
    in mtDNA 62
    and protein detection 34–36
    in sequences 45, 46
population genetics 39, 63–65
postmortem interval (PMI) 11, 135–137
preliminary examinations xvi, 77–89
preponderance of the evidence 125
President's DNA Initiative 120
primer 67, 68, 101
primer annealing 68
probability 39

probe 72, *73*, 101
prostatic antigen 85
protein 32, 34, 43, 51, 57, 88
proteinase K 96
protein synthesis 43, 57, *59*
pupa 11, 133
puparium 11
putative father 125

Q

Quanti-Blot 98–99, *99*
quencher 101
questioned specimen 7

R

race, and DNA typing 64–65
radioactive phosphorus 103
randomly applied polymorphic DNA
      (RAPD) 14
real-time PCR (RT-PCR) 89, 99,
      101–102
recidivism 115
recombination *54*, 55
reconstruction 89–94
red blood cell 23
repeat-sequence DNA 46, 47
restriction endonuclease 65
restriction enzymes 65, *66*, 103
restriction fragment length polymor-
      phism (RFLP) *104, 105*
   dot-blot typing *vs.* 108
   as first generation of DNA typing 48,
      100, 102–106
   restriction enzymes and 65
ribosome 58, 59
RNA (ribonucleic acid) 43, 57
RT-PCR. *See* real-time PCR

S

saliva 21, 27, 30–32, 85–86
SANEs (sexual assault nurse
      examiners) 82
Schütze, Nadine 21

SDIS (State DNA Indexing System) 117
secretor 27–29
Seebeck, Erich 136, 138–139
segregation 52
semen 20, 27–32, 80–81, 85
seminal fluid 20
September 11, 2001, terrorist attacks
      128
sequencing 45
serum protein polymorphisms 34–35
sex chromosomes 52
sexual assault cases
   ABO typing 27–32
   best evidence 78–79
   DNA profile databases 116–117
   DNA test result interpretation 123,
      125
   evidence collection 81–85, 87. *See
      also* semen
   forensic entomology 137–139
   future issues 147
   Y-chromosome markers 114
sexual assault nurse examiners (SANEs)
      82
short tandem repeat (STR) 108–111,
      112, 113, 114
single nucleotide polymorphism (SNP)
      131, 147
singleplex PCR 109
Siracusa, Vittorio 24
size ladder 100
skeletal remains 128–130
SNP. *See* single nucleotide polymorphism
Southern, Edwin 71
Southern blotting 71, *73*, 103
species testing 8, 87–89
specimens, selection of 77–79
spectrophotometry 97
spermatozoa 20, 85, *86*, 114
Sphaeralcea pollen 142
spoilage 77
State DNA Indexing System (SDIS) 117
STR. *See* short tandem repeat

Sturtevant, A. H. 42
succession 136
Sung Tz'u 16–17
swipe pattern 93

T

T (thymine) 55, 57
Takayama, Masao 18
tandem repeat. *See also* short tandem
    repeat; variable number of tandem
    repeats
    and DNA polymorphism 45
    and DNA typing 47–48, 50, 60
    and RFLP typing 100, 102
Tatum, E. L. 42
Teichmann, Ludwig 18
temperature, and insect life cycles 11,
    133–136
TF (transferrin) 35
thermal cycler 68
thermostable polymerase 68
throughput 147–148
thymine (T) 55, 57
toxicology 11, 18, 137
"trace and transfer" evidence xvii, 141–145
trace evidence 12, 13, 15
transcription 57, 58
transfer, forensic botany and 141
transferrin (TF) 35
transfer RNA (tRNA) 57–59
translation 58
triplet 57, 58
tRNA (transfer RNA) 57–59
typing (defined) 100

U

U (uracil) 57

Uhlenhuth, Paul 21
unknown 7, 27
unknown soldiers, identification of 130
uracil (U) 57
urea 21, 86
urine 21, 84, 86
Utz, Paul J. 18

V

vaginal secretions 20–21, 30, 81–85
variable number of tandem repeats
    (VNTR) 100, *103,* 108, 115–116
Venter, Craig 45

W

Washing Away of Wrongs (Sung Tz'u)
    16–17
Wassermann, August von 21
Watson, James 43, 55
Weinberg, Wilhelm 63
Wilkins, Maurice 55
wipe pattern 93
World Trade Center terrorist attacks (2001)
    128
wrongful convictions 123

X

X chromosome 52

Y

Y chromosome 52
Y-chromosome markers 111, 114–115

Z

zymogram *35,* 36